Lolita

THE BOOK OF THE FILM

Other Titles in the Applause Screenplay Series

Jacob's Ladder by Bruce Joel Rubin

∽

Fear and Loathing in Las Vegas: The Screenplay
by Terry Gilliam & Tony Grisoni

∽

The Battle of Brazil by Jack Mathews

∽

The Adventures of Baron Munchausen:
by Terry Gilliam and Charles McKeown

∽

Fisher King by Richard LaGravanese

∽

A Fish Called Wanda
by John Cleese and Charles Crichton

∽

Terminator 2: Judgment Day: The Book of the Film
by James Cameron and William Wisher

∽

JFK by Oliver Stone and Zachary Sklar

∽

William Goldman: Four Screenplays

∽

William Goldman: Five Screenplays

∽

Absolute Power by William Goldman

∽

The Ghost & the Darkness by William Goldman

∽

The Collected Screenplays of Paddy Chayefsky
(2 volumes)

AN ADRIAN LYNE FILM

Lolita
THE BOOK OF THE FILM

STEPHEN SCHIFF

BASED ON THE NOVEL BY
VLADIMIR NABOKOV

FOREWORD BY
JEREMY IRONS

PREFACE BY
ADRIAN LYNE

APPLAUSE
NEW YORK • LONDON

AN APPLAUSE ORIGINAL

Lolita: The Book of the Film
By Steven Schiff

Copyright © 1998 by Alphatex, F.A.
Excerpts from the novel "Lolita" copyright © 1955 by Vladimir Nabokov
The edition by arrangement with the Estate of Vladimir Nabokov

Library of Congress Cataloging-in-Publication Data

LC Catalog # 98-86581

ISBN: 1-55783-354-0

APPLAUSE BOOKS
211 West 71st Street
New York, NY 10023
Phone: (212) 496-7511
Fax: (212) 721-2856

10   9   8   7   6   5   4   3   2   1

CONTENTS

DEDICATION

To those who made it happen:

Adrian Lyne

Lili and Richard Zanuck

Tina Brown and Henry Finder

and, as always, Rebecca and Allegra

FOREWORD

This is a story that many people imagine they will find distasteful, especially in these days where the subject of pedophilia is so much in the public consciousness. I believe, however, that it has a place both as a piece of literature and as a film script. In today's society if we cannot understand human behavior, then how can we change it? How can we judge it? How can we educate our children about it?

The scope of Nabokov's story is as much about his relationship as a European, with this new, young, exciting country of America. Humbert Humbert, a rather weak and misguided man, steps outside our society's morality and for that he is punished. There are many levels on which to view the film. This script is merely the map of the film's landscape. It is a film which I believe should rest among the best of American cinema. It should be judged for what it is by a mature audience. Art, and I include cinema in that, should make us question and test our values and make us understand why we have the laws we do.

—Jeremy Irons

PREFACE

Of the seven films that I have directed, *Lolita* has been the true love of my life. But she has also been a cruel mistress. Before Stephen Schiff appeared from nowhere to write the script that I finally filmed, I had already been working on the project for some five years. I had no idea that, once the film was finished, it would take nearly that long again before anyone could get a glimpse of it. Although I knew that the film might be controversial, nothing prepared me (or anyone else involved in its making) for the outrageous response it received: the condemnations by people who had never seen the film, the hand-wringing by those who believed that to show a thing is the same as endorsing it, the de facto banning of the film by every studio in Hollywood — even those who, from the other side of their mouths, were telling me it was the best film I had made.

I believe it is. It is a film marked by my love for the book and for the America it depicts and for the doomed, twisted romance at its heart. In many ways, making *Lolita* was as great an experience as watching its fate unfold has been a disheartening one. In any case, the screenplay you hold in your hands is a kind of talisman of that experience, and so, to me, a kind of treasure.

My memories of working with Stephen Schiff are very fond. It was one of the best working relationships I have had with a writer. We both came to this book with the same respect and understanding, though we came from very different angles — his largely literary and even scholarly, mine visual and emotional; he a first-time screenwriter excited by the novelty of writing something beautiful in a new form, the screenplay; I aware of the medium's snags and limitations, but also re-excited, if you will, by his freshness and optimism.

Some of Stephen's best scenes — some of my favorites, in fact — could not make it to the final film, but this is the way of movies. I am glad, for Stephen and for you, that they are all here, preserved in these pages, and that our *Lolita,* too, lives on.

—Adrian Lyne
Provence
June, 1998

INTRODUCTION

This is the story — part of it, anyway — of a film that, whether you actually like it or not, certainly must be talked about in superlatives. The new $58-million movie version of *Lolita*, which I wrote and Adrian Lyne directed, has been the most controversial film of its moment. It has also been, until now, the most famous unreleased film in history — the most talked-about, the most written-about, the most notorious movie no one had ever seen. By the time it appeared before the American public for the first time, on the Showtime channel in August, 1998, it also enjoyed the very dubious honor of being the most expensive movie ever to have its U.S. premiere on television. *Lolita* has been hailed as the finest film its very successful director has ever made, and as a faithful, moving, carefully crafted rendition of a difficult and convoluted masterpiece. It has also been denounced as dull and purposeless, and, worse, as a danger to society, an incitement to pedophilia, an example of the breakdown of public morals.

As it happens *Lolita* was also my first screenplay. How did I, of all people, come to write it?

Most of my writing career had been spent as a journalist — a cultural critic, I suppose, pontificating about books, theatre, ballet, and, especially, about film. I had been a correspondent on a national television show, CBS's *West 57th*, and, by 1990, which is when this story properly begins, many people knew me as the "Critic at Large" (so to speak) of *Vanity Fair* magazine, where I had been writing film reviews and also critical profiles on everyone from Mikhail Baryshnikov to Vaclav Havel, from Jack Nicholson to Tom Stoppard. And a certain number of people knew me from the film reviews I delivered every week on Terry Gross's National Public Radio show, "Fresh Air." All of which provided a life sufficiently comfortable that the tales of perfidy and betrayal which echoed from the universe of screenwriters marked that career as a temptation easily overcome. Besides, I didn't consider it writing. (I was quite mistaken.) And then, too, just because you can write and you know movies doesn't mean you can write movies. Whenever I probed my cerebral cortex for the screenwriter lurking there, I kept bumping into the journalist.

Among those who regularly exhorted me toward screenwriting, there was only one I really trusted — and not only did I trust the producer-director Lili Fini Zanuck (who, with her producer husband, Richard Zanuck, had won the 1989 Best Picture Oscar *for Driving Miss Daisy*), she had been the best of best friends for several years. If anyone deserves credit for inventing me as a screenwriter, it is Lili. In 1990, the literary agent Irving Lazar (known as Swifty, a sobriquet he despised) was optioning properties on behalf of the Vladimir Nabokov estate, and Lili told me she thought I would be the perfect person to write a screen adaptation of *Lolita*.

Lolita is one of the most beautiful, poignant, funny, splendidly designed, gorgeously written, and psychologically acute works in the English language. To my mind, it is the greatest American novel of the postwar era. So the opportunity — if opportunity this was — to create a coherent artistic response to it was irresistible.

I got to work, but, I hasten to add, I did so idiotically: I wrote some forty pages of screenplay, but it was all dialogue, no "stage direction." I was impatient with the idea of describing what people did instead of what they said; wherever they were supposed to do something besides talk, I wrote, "Stage directions TK" (TK is American journalese for "to come.") I now know that what this approach signified was that I didn't know a damn thing about screenwriting, since screenwriting is actually about envisioning the movie in your head and capturing it as it goes by; the distinction between dialogue and stage direction is a phony one.

Still, I was somewhat saddened when, a few weeks later, Lili called me back and said, rather presciently, "Forget about it. In this political environment, any version of *Lolita* would be too controversial. It'll never get made."

End of story? For a while. I abandoned my misbegotten script and went on with my life. In 1992, *Vanity Fair*'s editor, Tina Brown, was hired to take the reins of *The New Yorker*, and she asked me to come with her — which I was more than happy to do. Screenwriting's nets and lures were not so much as an afterthought. Still, I experienced a twinge when I read that the director Adrian Lyne was indeed planning to make *Lolita*, and that he had hired James Dearden (who wrote Lyne's hit *Fatal Attraction*) to do the screenplay. Then I read that Lyne had decided not to film the Dearden screenplay and had hired the great English playwright and sometime screenwriter Harold Pinter.

Finally, in the fall of 1994, I received a call from Lili's husband, Richard Zanuck, who was now the producer of Adrian Lyne's *Lolita* project.

"Lili says you might have written some pages a few years ago." Dick said. "Send them. This movie's about to die."

So I did. Days, not weeks, passed. Another phone call from Dick Zanuck. "Stephen, we liked your pages," he said.

"My pages are ridiculous," I said.

"Well, I think they show us something," he said. "Now, here's what you do. Take the cheapest car you can find to the airport. Get the cheapest plane ticket available from New York to Los Angeles. Book the worst room in town. And come for a meeting with me and Adrian Lyne." And then the punch line. "Uh, you might not be reimbursed."

As I understand it, what was happening was this. The film belonged to Carolco, the big, flamboyant production company that had been run by Mario Kassar and Andy Vajna; it had made the "Terminator" movies, *JFK*, and all sorts of other blockbusters, good and bad. Now it was going bankrupt. Harold Pinter's *Lolita* script was being shown to various studios and distribution companies, but all of them were reacting very cautiously, and with good reason — Pinter's script, as fluent as it was, was also icy and off-putting; on the very first page, the protagonist, Humbert Humbert, warns us that he is a moral leper, and then proceeds to spend the film being one. The first solution that had come to everyone's mind was to hire a light and likable actor to compensate for the character's malignancy in the screenplay — Hugh Grant was the name most frequently invoked. But, old pros that they were, Zanuck and Lyne knew that casting was not going to solve the problem on the page. Still, with the company that owned the property going bankrupt, any real solution was going to have to be cheap. Seen in that light, asking me to fly to Hollywood was a brilliant stroke. I might not save the film, but then again I might. And God knows I was cheap.

I went. The meeting took place in Zanuck's office in Beverly Hills. The first thing he and Adrian wanted to know was whether I could see my way clear to setting the film in the present. (Unbeknownst to me, that was what Dearden's script had done.) The answer was "No." A *Lolita* growing up in America in this day and age would have been warned about the Humberts of the world from the age of three; her teachers would have talked to her about pedophiles; her mother would have been on the lookout. Besides, to set Nabokov's story in the present is to lose much of what it is about, for this was not just a novel about a grown man's love affair with his twelve-year-old stepdaughter, it was about the dawning impingement on the European mind of postwar America. It was about how the refined Old World fell into the thrall of the vulgar, beautiful, immature, and undeniably powerful young America that emerged from the Second World War. Nabokov set his novel in 1947, a singular moment in American cultural history — years before the finny, funny Fifties; before the invention of the great American teenager and the distinct consumer culture that sprang up to serve it. It was an America that had not been fully explored in the movies, and Nabokov had pinned and mounted it in the perfect pages of his novel.

We talked. An hour turned into a day. I was asked to stay another day, but I told them that the audition was over, and I returned home to New York. A few weeks later, we met in New York, in Adrian's room in the St. Regis Hotel. More shooting the shit, equally enjoyable. But Adrian kept leaping up and going into another room to make phone calls. He was hiring David Mamet to write the screenplay of *Lolita*.

As I reconstruct it now, I think Adrian must have liked what I was saying but could not imagine allowing his dream project to depend on me, for I was as green as they come. What does Dick Zanuck owe this guy?, he must have thought. Yet when I heard that Mamet had been hired, it did not strike me as a terrible setback. David Mamet's *Lolita*? As splendid as Mamet was and is, nothing in his lifelong portrayal of the American urban-male vernacular seemed to me to have anything to do with what this project needed. In short, I had a gut feeling that he might produce something amazing, but he was unlikely to produce the script that would get the movie made.

So I kept writing, on spec, and at an alarming speed. Never had I felt such pleasure in sitting down at the computer and banging it out. And this time, unlike when I had tried it back in 1990, what was coming through me was a movie. In my head I was seeing scenes, not just words; characters, not just dialogue. The thing flowed.

It took me about three weeks. I waited. Zanuck called to tell me that Mamet's script had not worked out. I told him that I had something to show him. I sent it in.

And then: the stretch limo came, the first-class plane ticket to LA, the room at the Four Seasons Hotel, complete with fruit basket. Suddenly I was living a satire of Hollywood.

But what had I written?

Right from the beginning, it was clear to all of us that this movie was not a "remake" of Stanley Kubrick's 1962 adaptation (which had a screenplay credited to Nabokov himself, though almost nothing of his script made it to the screen). In fact, most among our company actually looked upon the Kubrick version as a kind of "what not to do." (Nabokov himself famously likened the experience of seeing Kubrick's film to taking in a view of the countryside — as a patient in the rear of a speeding ambulance.) I had somewhat fonder memories of it than that, but I had not seen it for maybe fifteen years, and I didn't allow myself to go back to it again. My source material was the novel itself. Yet as much as I had always loved that novel, I also knew I would have to throw away a lot of it — even some of what I loved best.

Not long ago my friend Jason Epstein, the eminent Random House editor (who had helped get Nabokov's novel published in America) publicly pooh-poohed the idea of our adaptation (sight unseen, of course), saying that the beauty of *Lolita* resided in its style, and that, since a movie could capture only the book's paltry plot, such a project would scarcely be worth pursuing. This was an uncharacteristic statement from Jason, because Jason is usually brilliant and insightful, and on this particular subject he was being dumb. In the first place, *Lolita* would not be the masterwork it is if style were merely surface, artifice, frippery. Nabokov's style infuses not just the tone of the book, but its substance as well. (At its best, as in *Lolita*, style *is* substance.) No faithful film rendering of the book could fail to reflect the way Nabokov's style seeps into the characterizations, into the dialogue, into the imagery, into the plot itself. Besides, Nabokov was not just a great stylist, he was a master plotter — the story he constructs in *Lolita* is itself a fantastic yarn, pieced together with devilish skill. And all the more so, because the whole thing is filtered through the consciousness of one of the most singular and demented characters in literary history — Humbert Humbert.

Humbert is thoroughly equipped for greatness, and yet he winds up in an ignominy of his own making. Part of his tragedy — and a large part of his comedy — is that his enormous intelligence is always defeated by his obsession. He can't get outside that obsession to see who Lolita is, to see that she is actually a fairly ordinary little girl, more charming than some and probably more sexually precocious than most, but still a child. Humbert's world is completely internal, a world of language and fantasy. But in the movie I had to externalize it. The ornate curlicues of Nabokov's prose, which are so gratifying to dip and slide with on the page, simply couldn't work in a movie; in the mouth of a flesh-and-blood actor they would sound pretentious, precious, or absurd. The best one could do is hint at them — and, even then, one would have to proceed with caution.

As for the dialogue itself — well, there is surprisingly little of it in the novel. Nabokov is likely to hint at what is being said only in a line or two, such as, "I launched upon a hilarious account of my Arctic adventures." So the screenwriter has to make up that "hilarious account" out of thin air — noting, of course, that it may not be as hilarious as Humbert pretends. Where Nabokov does provide dialogue, his ear for the rhythms of American adolescent speech circa 1947 is not always perfect. In the end, an enormous amount of the dialogue in this screenplay appears nowhere in the book — though it has been fascinating to note the degree to which film critics think I've simply lifted it from the novel's pages. Another thing. Because Nabokov's Humbert lives in a kind of exalted subjectivity, Lolita herself is so much a figment of his imagination that she barely exists on the page. In effect, I had to reinvent her, piecing her together from my own adolescence and from adolescents I knew. Adrian had reared a daughter, and he remembered being fascinated by the world of things she inhabited — foods, toys, clothes, and so forth. I began thinking about the uniquely twisted and passionate relationships American girls often have with food; hence all the scenes with Oreo cookies and Wonder Bread and bananas and jawbreakers — none of which are in Nabokov's book (and many of which, sadly, were cut from the final film). What, after all, might this little girl be made of? That was the question.

I also had to create a relationship between Lolita and Humbert, a relationship that the book's completely unreliable narrator, Humbert himself, allows us only glimpses of. There is a moment, for instance, during Humbert and Lolita's cross-country travels, in which they are, in effect, a couple — a very odd couple (as Adrian called them), but a couple nevertheless. Nabokov leaves that mostly to the reader's imagination, but I felt I could not, and some of the most vivid scenes in the movie are those in which these two are on the road together, testing each other, confounding each other, and, yes, loving each other. (Perhaps it doesn't quite go without saying that our version is sexually much franker than the Kubrick version, in which nothing more erotic passes between Humbert and Lolita than a peck on the cheek. But it is my feeling that sexuality plays approximately the same role in our screen version as in the book, and is no more nor less emphasized.)

Almost from the beginning, it seemed to me that Adrian's conception of Humbert was absolutely right: that we have to sympathize with and, yes, love him even though his deeds revolt us. After all, that is very much what Nabokov accomplished — and what, arguably, much of the greatest literature has always brought about: by drawing us into a human soul, and by using our affections to do so, the writer initiates us into a deeper understanding not only of mankind at his finest but also of mankind at his most iniquitous.

I resorted to several approaches. First, Humbert had to be funny, charming, ironic, even roguish. I had to let him wink at the audience from time to time, and I did so in a variety of ways: in lines that have ironic double meanings, in intimate voice-overs, in instances of awkward or embarrassing behavior (like the way he examines his paunch in the mirror in the middle of a fight with Lolita). And there was another important step in humanizing Humbert: just as Nabokov did, Adrian and I wanted to link his obsession with Lolita to the nymphet who started it all when Humbert was only thirteen — his lost love, Annabel. Then I cemented the link with the scene in which Humbert tells us, in voice-over, "The shock of her death froze something in me. The child I loved was gone, but I kept looking for her — long after I had left my own childhood behind. . . ."

In the world of screenplay development, there is an invidious term that makes me flinch whenever it enters the conversation — and it does at every "story meeting." I am referring to "character arc." A movie character can't spend his allotted two hours of screen time being inert; he has to change, to develop — to put it disgustingly, he has to learn something. I hate this rule, and yet it is one of the great principles of narrative. A character without an arc is in grave danger of being merely a sitcom figure. (In fact, one of the things that distinguishes sitcoms from movies is that sitcom characters have static traits and impulses from which they keep acting, week after week. No one on *Seinfeld* had an arc.) In *The Iliad*, Achilles had an arc. Othello, Macbeth, Hamlet, and Lear had arcs; Michael Corleone had an arc; so did Bonnie and so did Clyde.

Humbert, too, needed an arc. Without resorting to schmaltz and without slamming the audience over the head, I had to show how he grows from the tormented, needy soul he is at the beginning to someone who has learned how to love — and who, in the end, is profoundly remorseful for what he has done to Lolita. The arc begins with his deviousness and self-absorption when he is living in the house of Charlotte Haze and culminates in three key moments, the first two of which I invented for the movie: Humbert's asking Lolita if she can ever forget what he did to her (he knows that she can never forgive him); his telling Quilty that he must kill him because, in stealing Lolita away, Quilty has cheated Humbert of his redemption; and, finally, the movie's last voice-over (a pastiche from the book), in which he proves his love for Lolita and symbolically returns to her the childhood that he has robbed.

One more thing. *Lolita* is not just a book, it is a puzzle. No one who reads it once can get it all; it was meant to be read at least twice, and, when it is, its various tricks and motives — especially the ones involving Quilty — make themselves clear. But I had to write a movie that an audience could take in entirely the first time. And this is tricky stuff. Stanley Kubrick avoided the problem completely by making Peter Sellers's largely improvised portrayal of Quilty dominate the movie (I've often thought his film should have been called *Quilty*). Kubrick begins with Quilty's murder, so the audience knows exactly who the shadowy nemesis is from the beginning. I wanted to try something more Nabokovian, and I hope that the effect of Quilty's mysterious appearances in the screenplay at least modestly approximates the effect of his dazzling encroachments on Humbert's life in the novel.

We rolled toward production. Actors were discussed for Humbert, but we always came back around to the obvious choice, Jeremy Irons. Melanie Griffith was cast as Charlotte Haze, Lolita's mother, and that seemed perfectly right to me, because I had conceived Charlotte as a woman whom every man in the room would want to sleep with except the one who could — Humbert. Casting Lolita was tougher. It was an enormous, difficult role, and we wanted to avoid, above all, the mistake that we felt Kubrick had made in casting Sue Lyon, a fifteen-year-old who nevertheless looked like a twenty-year-old hooker. Our Lolita was really going to be about a grown man's obsession with a child, not about a grown man's obsession with a hot young chick.

A six-month search ensued. Open casting calls. Mothers thrusting their daughters forward. Plump 30-year-olds assuring the famous director that they could pass as preadolescents. And then Adrian received a videotape in the mail: a kid from Malibu, whose only film performance had been as a stunt double, sent in footage of herself doing scenes from Nabokov's book. She wasn't quite beautiful, and she certainly wasn't polished, but Adrian saw immediately that she was enormously gifted — at once a seductress and a little girl. Dominique Swain was fourteen then (fifteen by the end of filming), but could easily pass for younger. She was Lolita.

Someone once said that a screenwriter on the set feels like a whore who's already been paid but keeps waiting around for breakfast. There was no real need for me to visit the numerous sets of *Lolita*, but, hell, they were filming a movie that I wrote, and I wanted to be there. Adrian was always hospitable, and it was lovely to watch Jeremy, Dominique, Melanie, and Frank Langella (who was magisterial as Quilty) mouthing my lines. Yet there were unsettling signs. I had been on film sets before, but on this one there seemed to be armies of people for even the smallest, most intimate scene. What were they all there for? Weather troubles plagued the first week of production. The original cinematographer was for some reason shooting dark, green, ugly footage, and he had to be replaced. (Howard Atherton, who then became the movie's cinematographer, did a knockout job.) Melanie got sick. Costs were mounting. *Lolita* wasn't going to be a low-budget film.

And yet by the end of the shoot, there was a real exhilaration in the air. Everyone knew that Adrian was getting something remarkable, that Jeremy was giving the performance of his life, and that Dominique was going to surprise the world. The dailies — the developed, uncut footage of what had been shot the previous day — were gorgeous: moving, shocking, funny, and sometimes hair-raising. When we saw the first lusty kiss between Lolita and Humbert, we all squirmed in our seats, and that was exactly as it should have been. If this film didn't from time to time make an audience acutely uncomfortable, we weren't doing our job.

Discomfort had come with the territory. Periodically, as we worked on the script, Adrian would suddenly succumb to a wave of paranoia: "They're going to have my ass," he would moan. "They're going to hound me from the theaters, lock me up and throw away the fucking key, man." At times I seemed to be the only one connected with the film who didn't harbor visions of some small-town sheriff descending on the set and carting us off to jail on obscenity charges, child pornography charges, or just general principle. During the shoot, we played by the strictest rules the film's lawyers could devise. Any nudity required an adult body double for Dominique. If Dominique sat on Jeremy's lap, a board was inserted between them. Dominique's mother and tutor were on the set whenever she was. I often found myself in the position of reassuring everyone: We're not going to be arrested, for Chrissake. This isn't the Fifties. We're not making a pornographic film. We're adapting one of the acknowledged great works of 20th century literature.

So I said. And so I thought.

In Washington, D.C., there resides a man named Orrin Hatch, who, throughout a long senatorial career, has consistently served as a small, pointy vector of maleficence. In 1996, as we were editing our movie, he saw to it that a rider was attached to a common spending bill. This rider, known as the Child Pornography Prevention Act of 1996, was aimed at a new breed of child pornographers who haunted the internet, using computer graphics to graft children's heads onto naked adult bodies in various erotic combinations, so that it looked as though children were having sex. To combat this admittedly tawdry scourge, Mr. Hatch's bill made it illegal (and punishable by long prison terms) for anyone to make any visual depiction that was "or appeared to be" a child having explicit sex, whether or not a child was actually involved.

Suddenly, we were in trouble.

The law was enacted as *Lolita* was being edited. It was so vaguely worded that it seemed to me certifiably unconstitutional, although a judge later upheld it. Broadly interpreted, it could have resulted in the banning of any number of mainstream films, paintings, book covers, photographs, MTV videos, and so forth. We didn't even know about it until Adrian read about it somewhere and went into a panic. And the panic was contagious.

By that time, the financiers of the film were a gigantic French corporation called Chargeurs, which then spun off a film distribution company called Pathé. In the throes of bankruptcy, Carolco had sold them its prize property, *Lolita*, and Chargeurs, looking at how well Adrian Lyne's films had always done worldwide (especially his sexy *9 1/2 Weeks*), had been certain that he was making the sort of blockbuster that any American studio would pay a premium to distribute. (Never mind that what I had written, and what Adrian was filming, was essentially an art film, albeit a very polished one.) Now the film's budget had ballooned, and on top of that, there was this zany new law. *Lolita*, presumably, might make a likely high-profile target for some ambitious US attorney or, again, some righteous small-town sheriff. (For days on end our heads bulged with visions of Rod Steiger in *In the Heat of the Night*.) So Pathé hired a law firm that specialized in obscenity law and showed it a rough cut of the film. And when the assembled attorneys saw the rough cut, the panic spread.

Adrian called me from the editing room in Santa Monica, feeling, as he often did in those days, ganged-up upon. The least Draconian of the assembled lawyers had been hired to vet the film, but he sounded Draconian enough to me. And his word was going to be final. He had been hired not just to ensure that nothing in *Lolita* was culpable under the Child Pornography Prevention Act, but also that nothing in it would incite those US attorneys and small-town sheriffs into even thinking about bringing action against it, and that, furthermore, it might be impervious to whatever laws zealous local authorities decided to cook up in the wake of the Child Pornography Prevention Act. At the moment, the film was provocative, certainly, but by no means porny. There was some nudity — all of it filmed with an adult body double — and a little of it was rather stirring, but none of it was essential, and, truth to tell, most of it struck me as a distraction. But for the lawyer, the nudity wasn't the half of it. He felt that there were sequences that could not be modified in any way that would make them acceptable — nudity or no nudity, they would have to be cut out of the film completely. And it made no difference that the film had just been shown to the MPAA ratings board, which gave it an R rating, with no hesitation, no requests for cuts or changes, no questions asked.

"This is ridiculous," I sputtered into the phone. "This lawyer wants to wreck our film because of a law that's probably unconstitutional and will certainly be thrown out the moment anyone tests it."

But that was the problem. *Lolita* was an obvious test case, and none of its makers wanted to be hauled into court even with the certainty of winning. The widely held view that such controversy inevitably translates into box office is simply wrong. (It didn't work for David Cronenberg's hotsy-totsy *Crash*, did it?) And the very real risk not only of grotesque lawyers' fees but of real jail time was enough to cow Adrian, the film's French owners, and the film's producers, who were now, since Richard Zanuck had left the film before production began, Mario Kassar and Joel Michaels.

On my shelves was a very interesting book that the editor Jason Epstein had given me: *Girls Lean Back Everywhere: The Law of Obscenity and the Assault on Genius*, by Edward de Grazia, a lawyer who had, according to the book, "been responsible for freeing from censorship Aristophanes's *Lysistrata*, Henry Miller's *Tropic of Cancer*, William Burroughs's *Naked Lunch*, and the Swedish film *I Am Curious — Yellow*." I called de Grazia and solicited his advice, and he armed me with details and precedents. I learned all about United States v. Knox and United States v. McCormick and New York v. Ferber, and I began to have a sense of where child pornography law stood at the moment. I called the film's producer Joel Michaels and said, "Let me come out there and talk to the lawyer."

"With all due respect, Stephen," he said, "you're no lawyer, and nothing you say is going to sway anybody."

I was only the writer, as they say. But Joel finally relented, and I flew to L.A.

Ladies and gentlemen of the jury, here is what you must never have in life: a lawyer in the editing room. Let's call him Larry. Larry was an affable, mustachioed man who badly wanted to be liked even though he was intent on raping our film. He called us "Colleagues." He would regale us with stories of his testimony before the Supreme Court, and as he waxed eloquent about his cases, it quickly became clear that Larry was a porn lawyer: his most famous client had been the underage porn actress Tracy Lords. Larry had a scarily intent way of watching the questionable sequences, which played on the video monitors in the darkened editing room. The look on his face and a certain tension in the body led me to believe that he was carefully monitoring his own physical responses: if we were getting a rise out of him, we had to cut. This method had nothing to do with any law I knew about, but the producers never tired of telling me I knew nothing anyway, and everyone wanted to make sure I understood that if Larry said something had to go, it had to go. Adrian rocketed from fear to despair to depression and back again, as Larry justified his obduracy by telling us that nothing he saw in the movie violated any law now, but that he had been charged with protecting us from laws that might arise later. He was terribly sorry, but what could he do?

We cut. Sometimes, I thought, the cuts actually helped the film. Crotch shots had to go, and, indeed, there was legal precedent for them to go, and their removal was fine with me. There was no legal precedent for the removal of breast shots, but we didn't really need breast shots — in any case, they went. What we did need, however, were two crucial scenes that Larry wanted to remove completely — no amount ot trimming, he felt, could reduce their impact. Of course, that was why we so wanted to keep them — they were powerful. One of them was the Comics Scene, in which Lolita reads comics (at the Sandman Motel) while she is sitting on Humbert's lap; as we watch, we realize that they are having sex. The other was the scene in which Lolita sneaks out of the motel while Humbert is in town shopping and getting a haircut; when he returns, they have a terrible fight that ends in the movie's most aggressive sexual encounter. Larry luridly called this the Rape Scene.

We snipped, we fudged, I played bad cop to Adrian's good cop, but nothing we did could budge Larry. The Comics Scene was about to bite the dust. Finally, Adrian and I reversed roles. He went into a high-pitched, half-mad tirade that was almost terrifying, an enraged-elephant rant that splattered the walls with warning and woe and artistic temperament. I knew such an outcry would never sway so chilly a creature as a lawyer, but it sure created a mood. And then, playing good cop, I stepped in. "Larry," I said, in my most reasonable tone, "let me ask you something. What does the statute say?"

"It says, Stephen, that we not only can't have any depiction of a child having explicit sex, we can't even have the *appearance* of a child having explicit sex," said Larry. "So even though these two might not be having sex in these scenes, if some US attorney thinks they *appear* to be —"

"What's the wording, Larry?" I asked.

"The act outlaws 'any visual depiction . . . where . . . such visual depiction is, or appears to be, of a minor engaging in sexually explicit conduct.' See, and that 'appears to be' is the point, because —"

"Larry," I said, "with all due respect, I have to tell you that you have misunderstood the statute."

"What?" he said.

"This law says nothing about what appears or doesn't appear to be explicit sex," I said. "The definition of 'sexually explicit conduct' remains what it has always been, and there's plenty of legal precedent that has established that." (I promise you I can talk this way when called upon.) "The words 'appears to be' don't refer to the sex," I continued. "They refer to the child. If there 'appears to be' a child engaged in sexually explicit conduct we're in trouble. But since there is no sexually explicit conduct in this scene, whether the person engaged in it appears to be a child or not doesn't matter. If there's no explicit sex, we haven't broken any law."

A long silence. Adrian was slack-jawed, the editors bleary-eyed. Larry shifted uncomfortably in his seat. "Let me look at the scene again," he said.

We ran the Comics Scene again. And this time, Larry said, "You know, I'm beginning to see all the changes you've made. I don't know why I missed them the first time. You know something? I think you guys have done it. I think I can live with this. Yeah, this is good. This is good."

Well, it wasn't good. Not really. The scenes had lost some of their rhythm, some of their power. But at least they stayed. And the Comics Scene is still often cited as the single most disturbing scene in the film.

We had lost other scenes, too, amid all the lawyering. But we had a cut we could live with. We previewed the movie three times in the Los Angeles area, and all three showings went smashingly. We continued to snip and adjust. With some trepidation, we screened the film for Dmitri Nabokov, the only child of Vladimir Nabokov and the cultivated, vigilant executor of his father's estate. He pronounced it "stunning," and later issued a statement: "The new *Lolita* is a sensitively conceived, beautifully produced film. Far from being the explicit shocker some feared and others craved, it achieves a cinematic dimension of poetry far closer to the novel than Stanley Kubrick's distant approximation. . . . Lyne's *Lolita*, . . . as well as Schiff's script, tend to let the viewer's fancy fend for itself, as Nabokov's prose did for the reader. . . . The latest *Lolita* is splendid."

Finally, in March 1997, two years after I had finished the screenplay, it was time to show the film to the would-be distributors, the studios.

What happened next was very strange. One by one, the studios saw the film. Many of the executives went out of their way to congratulate Adrian, to tell him that it was his best film ever, to recount in detail their ravishment over it, to beg him to work with them on his next film. And then, one by one, they refused to distribute it. "It's a really good movie," one studio head told the *Washington Post*, under cover of anonymity. "But it's not something we're going to pick up. It's a pretty difficult subject matter. It is tasteful, but it's still uncomfortable."

There are those among us who believe in uncomfortable art — who think, in fact, that if art isn't uncomfortable it isn't art. The grit that makes the pearl, the darkness at the heart of the seemingly frothiest comedies, the suspended dissonance amid the counterpoint — this is what thrills and exalts. But art, of course, wasn't the question. Some of the studio heads, I gather, genuinely didn't like the film, but for most that wasn't the question either. There were two questions. The first involved a reading of the cultural atmosphere into which *Lolita* was plunging. Never in history had there been such a horrified awareness of the pedophilia lurking around the fringes of American life. The Megan Kanka case, the JonBenet Ramsay case, the Polly Klass murder, the Belgian sex murders — all these were in the air. The Christian right had been fulminating for years on the subject of family values, smug moralists like William Bennett were talk-show regulars, and no film courted controversy without running into efficiently organized watchdog groups run by zealots like Donald Wildmon and others of his ilk. In Oklahoma, police had seized videotape copies of the Volker Schlondorff film *The Tin Drum*, accusing it of being child pornography — and its Academy Award for Best Foreign Film be damned.

Had we released *Lolita* in the 70s or 80s, I believe that it would have easily made its way into distribution. But the culture has contracted since then. And even if it hasn't, its gatekeepers believe it has. (Thus the gap between the alarm the gatekeepers expected us to feel over President Clinton's sexual shenanigans and the meager alarm we actually did feel.) Still, whether or not there would have been some vast surge of outrage upon the release of *Lolita*, the potential distributors certainly thought there would be. Every advance article about the film included threats from advocates of child welfare and family togetherness; newspaper columns railed against the project, sight unseen, from a vantage of laborious ignorance. Steve Dunleavy, chief mad dog of the *New York Post*, was typical: "We have kiddie porn sweeping computer networks — and too many JonBenets lying in tiny coffins. What on earth would prompt anyone to do a remake of a movie on the most forbidden of subjects? Don't give that art baloney as an excuse. . . . We don't need another *Lolita* to light more tinderboxes of madness."

By the time potential distributors saw it, *Lolita* already felt too risky. Especially since Pathé had ensured that the risk would be unreasonably large: the word was that they were demanding $25 million plus the cost of prints and advertising for the privilege of distributing the film domestically. I can't verify that figure, but I can say that Pathé certainly reduced its demands as time passed — to no avail. "I have piles of letters," Adrian told a reporter, "at least twenty or thirty from different people — agents and executives — who say how overwhelmed and moved they were by the picture. I've never had that. They say they've talked about the movie for days after; they tell me, 'It's your best work.' And suddenly they've become mute."

Months passed. Deals were almost made and then disappeared. We were down to the independent distributors, but just what did that mean? Miramax was part of Disney, and Disney, with its reputation and its stockholders, was never going to spring for *Lolita*. We heard that October Films, the distributors of *Secrets and Lies* and *The Apostle*, wanted it, but then they were bought by Universal, which was owned by Seagrams, which didn't want a *Lolita* on its hands. As word spread of the film's plight, all sorts of people and groups stepped forward — the New York Film Festival wanted to consider it; various critics and columnists offered to champion it. This time, however, it was Pathé who turned risk-averse. Their prize chickadee had turned into an albatross overnight, and now they became afraid of exposing it. What if the distribution deals they had already made in other countries turned sour because of the American reaction? What if the movie played in a film festival and got a bad review? Pathé was convinced that no amount of press support would sway American distributors, and so they decided simply to release *Lolita* in Europe first in the hope that the response there would prove so overwhelming that American distributors would change their minds.

To me, this plan seemed naive at best. Since when did American distributors look to Europe for guidance? *Lolita* would have to be a jaw-dropping blockbuster overseas to catch America's attention, and I knew that, no matter how kindly it was received, it was never going to be *Independence Day*. A wiser course, it seemed to me, might have been to self-distribute the film — either by forming our own distribution company (using experienced distribution people, of course) or even by four-walling the film — that is, by renting selected theaters, showing the movie, and hoping that the interest it drew would attract still more interest. In any case, if the film were going to open in Italy first (which indeed was the plan), how about a splashy premiere at the Venice Film Festival? Again, Pathé deemed the idea too risky — if it got bad reviews there, then its Italian opening might be marred.

In the end, the film premiered in September, 1997, at the San Sebastian Film Festival in Spain. Reviews were mixed. A Spanish critic sniffed, "With *Lolita*, [Lyne] has made his best film. It is not a good film. Neither is it bad. It is nothing." But Lee Marshall, the critic for the British trade publication *Screen International* said, "The US distributors who have refused to touch this story of illicit paternal passion have a lot to answer for. The film manages to be at once glossily watchable, psychologically complex, and morally mature — not something we always associate with Adrian Lyne's oeuvre. *Lolita* is his best yet — by quite a wide margin — and it even gives Stanley Kubrick's 1962 version a run for its money, largely thanks to screenwriter Stephen Schiff's intelligently faithful adaptation of Nabokov's novel." After the festival, the film opened in Italy and did exceptionally well, but it did less well in Spain. In Germany a few months later, protest groups rallied to try to stop its opening, and when they failed, they picketed movie theaters showing the film and leafleted moviegoers. Seeing *Lolita* in Germany was a little like trying to get an abortion in America. In England, its passage by the British Board of Film Classification (which decides whether films can be seen in Britain) was greeted with howls of protest.

Meanwhile, a handful of American critics were traveling the world trying to see the film. The trade paper *Variety* hated it: "The opening section works well. . . . But problems arise when the director succumbs to the urge to make An Adrian Lyne Film. . . . In lieu of real dramatic momentum or emotional weight, we get gratiuitous art directional flourishes." But Jack Kroll of *Newsweek* loved the film, saying, "Lyne has translated Nabokov's classic with sensitivity, intelligence, and style." Richard Schickel in *Time* magazine was equally kind, and Caryn James of the *New York Times* wrote a cover story for the Sunday "Arts and Leisure" section in which she called it "an eloquent tragedy laced with wit and a serious, disturbing work of art." On ABC's *Nightline*, she called it "one of the best movies I've seen all year."

All of which was nice to read, but it didn't change the situation. The movie had been, effectively, banned in America. Fear had triumphed. But fear of what? Reduced to its simplest terms, I suppose, the argument against releasing *Lolita* was that a man might walk into a movie theater, watch a rich, funny, sad, complicated movie that hammers home no message but does end in the complete undoing of a pedophile, and might then say, "Hey! Pedophilia! Great idea! Think I'll try it!" Absurd, but there you have it. It seems almost too obvious to point out that this is not the way human sexual psychology works. Isn't it apparent enough that a man who was already a pedophile might easily be stimulated by almost anything — *The Wizard of Oz*, *Lassie*, you name it? And that a man who was not a pedophile was not going to become one as a result of watching *Lolita*? Yet there are always those in our culture who believe that everything will be all right as long as we just keep our inner darkness under wraps. Expose nothing to the light. Violence will go away if no one sees it in the movies. Bad guys will stop committing sex crimes if the culture doesn't "give them ideas." Guns don't kill people, TV shows kill people. Etcetera.

The fate of *Lolita* the movie oddly parallels that of *Lolita* the book. Nabokov's great novel could find no American publishing house willing to take it on in 1954; in 1955, it was published in Paris by Olympia Press, a house best known for erotica. But it wasn't until Graham Greene championed *Lolita* by naming it one of the three best books of 1956 that anyone even took notice of it. France promptly banned it; the British columnist John Gordon called it "the filthiest book I have ever read," and it wasn't until 1958 that the book was published in America. It became an immediate best-seller.

Lolita the movie will enjoy a somewhat different fate. In the spring of 1998, in the oddest turn yet in a very odd story, the premium cable network Showtime bought all American rights to the film; it broadcast *Lolita* to men, women, and children of all ages in August, 1998; a smallish theatrical run may follow, and then, perhaps a wave of pedophilia. Perhaps you, dear reader, will examine my screenplay and find yourself subject to new, uncontrollable, illicit longings. But I doubt it. I hope you will at least laugh once in a while, and once in a while, perhaps, find yourself moved.

A NOTE ON THE PREVIOUS SCREENPLAYS

Although I was allowed to use, and even asked to use, material from the three earlier screenplays, there is almost nothing here from anyone else's script, with one exception: several moments came from Harold Pinter. This sort of attribution is difficult to make, since Adrian Lyne himself was so instrumental in winnowing and shaping material from the book, and both Pinter and I (and David Mamet, for that matter), worked from a detailed outline that Lyne devised. Nevertheless, Pinter invented several things on his own, and I'd like to point out just what they are. There are bits of stage direction and dialogue that I have surely missed in the accounting that follows, but the main purloinings from Pinter are these:

The dialogue about not eating peaches until the sun goes down is his, although it was cut from the final film. His, too, is the jabber on the porch about being a cook at the North Pole and about Charlotte's being too plump to be a ballerina. Pinter came up with Lolita's line, "What's a conscience? Whatever it is, I don't have one" (also not in the final film). And the line about Lolita's having washed her hair a couple of months ago is his as well. My favorite Pinter moment is the first couple of lines in the scene in which Charlotte is serving Humbert dinner; although the reference to "Gourmet" magazine is mine, Humbert's response to Charlotte's salad—"Perfectly judged"—is Pinter's, and very lovely. The cleric's funny lecture about how eternity goes on for a long, long time is Pinter's. So are the "sticks and whips" and the exquisite line "You'd have to knit things and sing hymns" during Humbert's warning about what would happen if Lolita went to the police. From Pinter, too, came "You look one hundred percent better when I can't see you" in one of the car scenes. And Pinter invented the lines about Humbert's depriving Lolita of her civil rights during the Beardsley sequence. He also came up with Reverend Rigger's dialogue, in the play rehearsal, about Lolita's becoming a witch. Finally, as Humbert and Lolita leave Beardsley, they talk about whether Clare Quilty is a man or a woman; this, too, is based on Pinter but was cut from the film.

ACKNOWLEDGMENTS

The people to whom this volume is dedicated deserve even more thanks here. If you have read my introduction, you get a sense of how instrumental Lili Zanuck was in making this screenplay happen. I wish only to add that she is the most adored of friends, and that without her, there would be not only no screenplay but no screenwriter. Richard Zanuck gave me the opportunity when no one else (except Lili, of course) could have conceived of such a thing. He is not only among the finest producers in Hollywood, he is a real movie man, a joy and an inspiration to work with.

I have said a lot about Adrian Lyne, but I want to emphasize once again that in many ways this script reflects his perspective as much as mine. It's true that much--perhaps most — of what is here is not, finally, in the film he directed, but it's also true that to many of the moments I invented Adrian brought a vision that I could never have mustered. He was my chief guide through the writing process, and his penchant for detail (which shows in every frame he shoots) made me feel as though I were in the hands of the most exacting of *New Yorker* editors. When he would call me on the phone, he would jokingly begin with, "Stephen, it's me. Your mentor." But it was no joke. He really was.

My other mentor was, and is, Tina Brown, first my editor at *Vanity Fair* and then my editor at *The New Yorker,* always my dear friend, my unflagging supporter, and someone to whom I truly owe everything. Because Tina is, by any objective measure, the great American magazine editor of the last two decades of this century, she is a very large target and hence, to my way of thinking, one of the most misunderstood people in American public life. To say that she is an editor of genius is to add nothing new to the conversation, but it may be worth saying that she is also warm, loyal, devoted, blazingly smart, drop-dead funny, and a terrific friend.

Equally smart, devoted, loyal, warm, and funny is Henry Finder, who is more direct-ly my editor at *The New Yorker,* and who did such a good job of making sure that I had space to, as he put it, "surprise" myself in the writing of this screenplay, that I consider him one of its midwives. He is that rare print editor who really understands screenplays, and his brainy but never too rarefied counsel is among the most valuable influences of my life.

Finally, let me thank those others who made both the movie and the book happen: my lawyer, Linda Lichter, who was much more than a lawyer on this project, since she was also my agent, my hand-holder, and my entire army — a superb woman warrior if there ever was one. Dmitri Nabokov offered moral and intellectual sustenance all along the way, and his defense of the film was gallant, eloquent, and kind. Nikki Smith, Dmitri's agent, virtually made the publication of this book happen by combined forces of generosity, understanding, and steely will; she is the best person in the universe to have on your side. Ed De Grazia, whom I have talked about at length in my introduction, armed me with the legal weapons I needed to battle those who wished to destroy the movie by defending it to death. Joel Michaels and Mario Kassar, the film's producers, fought the good fight until it practically broke them. Francois Ivernel, my main contact at Pathé, was always attentive, reasonable, and humane, and without him this book could not have happened. The cast and crew of the film will always hold a special place in my heart, especially Frank Langella, who has become a dear friend, and Jeremy Irons, the film's most fluent defender. Ronni Chasen and Melanie Hodal, the film's publicists, have made the best of one of the most peculiar situations any pub-licist has ever had to face. My CAA agents Robert Bookman, Jessica Tuchinsky, Bryan Lourd, and Joe Rosenberg have taken the little bit of career that Lolita gave them to work with and have run with it like champion milers, and I also include among that number two agents who have left my employ but were instrumental in getting me here: David Lonner, now at Endeavor, and Jay Moloney, whom I hope God will join me in blessing, wherever he is.

I feel I owe a thank you to those members of the American press — hence, in a way, my colleagues — who saw their way clear to defend this beleaguered film. I'm thinking par-ticularly of Jack Kroll, Caryn James, Richard Schickel, and Erica Jong. And, finally, to Allegra, the angel who keeps my entire landscape alight, and Rebecca, the woman who makes everything in my life possible except adequate acknowledgment.

FADE IN:

NEW ENGLAND COUNTRYSIDE — DAY (1950)   *A beat-up Fifties car, a Melmoth, driving slowly just outside a small town. It creeps over into the left lane, where it zig-zags very evenly. This is not the weaving of a drunk. The driver seems to be veering back and forth on purpose.*

We peer through the grimy front windshield — but we can't quite make him out. Cars come at him, then swerve into the opposing lane, honking brutally.

INTERSECTION IN A SMALL TOWN   *The light turns red, but the Melmoth sails through it.*

Inside the car, a bloodied gun sits on the seat next to Humbert. Humbert, a man of about forty: tall, movie-star handsome, with an air that would be distinguished if his face were not freckled with blood.

His hands on the steering wheel. Between his right thumb and index finger, a bobby pin.

> HUMBERT
> Lolita.

Close up on Humbert Humbert's eyes. They are aglow.

> HUMBERT
> Light of my life, fire of my loins. My sin, my soul.

Close up on his mouth.

> HUMBERT
> Lo-lee-ta.

HOTEL MIRANA — DAY (1920s) *The palmy grounds of the Hotel Mirana. A car driving up. Its well-heeled passengers — The Leighs — get out. Valets handle their bags.*

> HUMBERT'S VOICE
> But there might have been no Lolita at all had I not first met . . . Annabel.

Through the crowd we find Annabel, daughter of the Leighs, alighting from the taxi and looking around approvingly.

> HUMBERT'S VOICE
> She was twelve.

We glimpse her fleetingly through the crowd. Then we see that this is Humbert's point of view — he is watching her from the hotel steps.

> HUMBERT'S VOICE
> I was thirteen. And whatever happens to a boy during the summer he is thirteen can mark him for life.

A view of the hotel, as if in a photograph album.

> HUMBERT'S VOICE
> That hotel you see, the Mirana — that belonged to us.

Accompanying the next speech, a series of short, family-photo-style pictures.

> HUMBERT'S VOICE
> My father was half French and half Austrian. My mother was English. She lived long enough only to determine my accent, and then, when I was five, she died. Rather suddenly.

HILLSIDE — DAY *Under a bare, isolated tree, Humbert's mother is picnicking when she is abruptly — and comically — hit by lightning.*

HUMBERT'S VOICE
A chill crept into my life, and for years I thought nothing
could warm me again — until Annabel.

FRENCH RIVIERA BEACH — DAY *Young Humbert sits in the sand
with Annabel. Her parents tower above them several yards away,
snoozing in lounge chairs.*

HUMBERT'S VOICE
She wanted to be a nurse. I wanted to be a spy. All at
once, we were madly, hopelessly in love.

*They are hypnotized by each other. Annabel lets sand spill through
her fingers, and then her hand creeps through the sand toward
Young Humbert's. Their fingers touch. They steal a glance backward
at her parents, who are snoring in the sun. Annabel brings her bare
knee stealthily toward Young Humbert. It touches his thigh. They
glance back again at their overseers, and this time their sightline has
been blocked by some playing children. They kiss, but their pleasure
ends when some of the playing children crash into them and shower
them with sand.*

A CAVE — RIVIERA BEACH — DAY *Young Humbert peers in. He
hears rustling. As his eyes adjust to the light, he sees Annabel, who
is undressing — and looking at him.*

*She reaches under her dress, pulls off a pair of white cotton under-
pants tripped in blue ribbon, and tosses them in front of her.*

*Young Humbert goes toward her and picks up the underpants.
Kneeling, he slowly pulls out the blue ribbon. She takes his hand —
the one with the ribbon in it — and draws it toward her to help her
unbutton her dress.*

A red ball bounces in, followed by two bearded bathers.

BEARDED BATHER 1 (OFFSCREEN)
It went in — hello. Well, come on then! Go to it, lad! Go
on!

Young Humbert jumps up, trying to shield Annabel from the men, as she struggles to get back into her shorts.

HOTEL SUITE — NIGHT   *Looking through a window into the Hotel Mirana, watching the Leighs and two friends playing bridge.*

We move down the hotel's exterior, then over an expanse of lawn.

Finally, the ruins of a low wall in a mimosa grove. There, Young Humbert and Annabel are beginning to make love.

> HUMBERT'S VOICE
> On our last night together, we managed to escape to a
> mimosa grove, leaving her jailers upstairs to play bridge.

Young Humbert kisses Annabel's ears, the corner of her lips. As he reaches beneath her light dress, a dreamy and eery expression comes over her features. She trembles.

Her bare knees catch and compress his wrist

Her face — as she rubs her dry lips against his. She reaches down to grasp him as well.

HOTEL SUITE   *Mrs. Leigh shoots out of her seat.*

> MRS. LEIGH
> Where's Annabel?

OUTSIDE ON THE LAWN   *Mr. Leigh appears on the steps in front of the lawn.*

> MR. LEIGH
> Annabel! Where are you, girl?

Annabel and Young Humbert give each other a long, aching, loving look.

YOUNG HUMBERT'S FACE   *Distraught. He has been weeping.*

BEACH — WINTER   *Pewter skies and a wintry wind. Young Humbert stands alone, and we are behind him, looking toward the sea.*

> HUMBERT'S VOICE
> Four months later, she died of typhus. In Corfu.

A EUROPEAN PARK — DAY   *Grown-up Humbert is sitting on a park bench, pretending to read but actually watching young girls jumping rope, playing hopscotch, etc.*

> HUMBERT'S VOICE
> The shock of her death froze something in me. The child I loved was gone, but I kept looking for her — long after I had left my own childhood behind.

One of the girls comes over to Humbert's bench, props a foot on it next to him and leans over and fixes her rollerskate. Humbert watches with a little too much interest.

SUBWAY TRAIN   *Humbert in the Parisian Metro, basking in the aura of a young girl leaning over him to read a map on the wall, her curls dangling near his face.*

> HUMBERT'S VOICE
> The poison was in the wound, you see. And the wound wouldn't heal.

TRAIN — DAY (1947)   *Humbert in a train rolling through green American countryside.*

> HUMBERT'S VOICE
> I probably should have joined the priesthood. Instead I accepted a teaching post at Beardsley College in America. I had a summer free before the fall semester,

so I thought I'd finish the textbook I was working on — a survey of French literature for American students.

RAMSDALE STATION — DAY *Humbert on the train platform, heading through the station, and getting into a cab.*

> HUMBERT'S VOICE
> I took my advance and went to live with some old friends of my late uncle's, the McCoos, in the New England town of Ramsdale.

BURNT-OUT McCOO HOUSE — DAY *Humbert and McCoo stand before the burnt ruins of McCoo's house.*

> HUMBERT'S VOICE
> But on arriving I found that it was no longer there.

RAMSDALE STREETS — DAY *Humbert in an American taxi rolling along leafy, small-town streets, looking at a piece of paper with a number on it. In the background, a large dog stretching and getting to its feet.*

> McCOO'S VOICE
> No one was hurt, thank God. That's all that matters. The wife, you know, was out shopping. Buying some things for —

He is suddenly too moved to go on.

> HUMBERT'S VOICE
> Look, Mr. McCoo, don't worry about me. I'll just go back to New York. I can stay in my uncle's apartment until the new owners arrive.

> McCOO'S VOICE
> No, no, wouldn't hear of it. We've made arrangements for you. You can stay with Charlotte Haze. You'll like

Charlotte. She's a widow now, of course, poor thing.
Been wanting a boarder. Cheer her up to have a man
around the house again.

*The dog pursues the taxi, which swerves and screeches. In the back
seat, Humbert bumps his head on the door.*

LAWN STREET — DAY   *The taxi stops in front of a white-frame
house, the Haze house, and Humbert gets out, wrestles with luggage
and fare, goes to the door, and rings the bell. A black maid, Louise,
opens the door.*

> LOUISE
Just a minute. Something's burning.

*She rushes back into the house. Humbert steps in. The house is
bourgeois-arty, with souvenirs from Mexico everywhere. A print of
Van Gogh's "L'Arlesienne" is on the wall.*

> LOUISE
Miz Haze be down in a . . .

> CHARLOTTE (OFFSCREEN)
Is that Monsieur Humbert? I'll be down in one . . .

Charlotte is on the upper landing, leaning over the banister.

> LOUISE
She be down in one . . .

> CHARLOTTE
Monsieur Humbert?

*She arrives smoking and gesturing: shapely, blowsy, just past the
peak of a considerable attractiveness. We see the long ash at the
cigarette tip and we watch her tapping it. Ash flies everywhere.*

> HUMBERT
Yes. Uh, Mrs. Haze, is it?

Lolita

They shake hands. She picks a bit of tobacco from her tongue.

CHARLOTTE
Charlotte. I'm so pleased to make your acquaintance.
Frank McCoo told me all about your scholarly pursuits.
You know, I myself just cherish the French tongue.

HUMBERT
Mmmm. Could I — do you mind if I — ?

CHARLOTTE
Oh, sit down, Professor Humbert. I'm being so thought-
less. Drink?

HUMBERT
No, thanks. Really can't stay.

CHARLOTTE

Don't be silly.

They sit. Humbert gets up, extracts an apple core he has sat on, and places it in an ashtray, which is overflowing with butts.

CHARLOTTE

Humbert Humbert. I was going to ask you — it's an unusual name.

HUMBERT

Yes, isn't it? My father had rather an odd sense of humor.

CHARLOTTE

Well, I can tell you're going to adore Ramsdale. You're going to fit right in. We've got Hourglass Lake just up Route 17, and Tuesday night's our theater group. No less a personage than Clare Quilty — you know, the play-wright? He gave us a reading last week. And that's not uncommon — his brother, Ivor, is our dentist here. Oh, and we've got Great Books on alternate Thursdays. But I guess you probably know them all by heart. Maybe you'd like to be a guest speaker?

HUMBERT

I tell you, Mrs. Haze —

CHARLOTTE

Charlotte.

HUMBERT

Charlotte. I'm so awfully tired. Perhaps we could just look at the room, and then . . .

CHARLOTTE

Oh, I'm so sorry. I just — well, let's do the tour. Living room —
(she burps)
— excuse me. You've seen the living room. These things are mostly Mexico . . .

She picks up a stray sock and stuffs it in a pocket.

> CHARLOTTE
> *(calling out)*
> Louise, have you cleaned in here?
> *(to Humbert)*
> Harold and I — the late Mr. Haze — we adored Mexico.
> The whole idea of a culture that sophisticated — and we
> think of *them* as primitive. I mean, look at us!

> HUMBERT
> Indeed. Yes.

> CHARLOTTE
> Upstairs. And this is your room. Space for a desk — any-
> thing you want. And at $20 a month, you can't beat the
> price . . .

HAZE HOUSE — UPSTAIRS   *They pass bedroom doors and a bathroom, with limp wet things overhanging the dubious tub, a hair curl
inside it, a rubber shower hose, and a pinkish cozy covering the toilet
lid.*

> CHARLOTTE
> Over here, these are our rooms. And here's the bathroom
> — sorry, a little messy. I don't mind mess; it's filth I can't
> stand. But Louise takes care of that. Oh! Speak of *le dia-
> ble*!

> LOUISE
> I'll go now, Mrs. Haze.

> CHARLOTTE
> Yes, Louise, all right. Did I pay you? I'll pay you Friday?

> LOUISE
> That's all right.

They go back downstairs.

> CHARLOTTE
> Kitchen. And if you have any special food needs, you just
> say. Well, I don't know if Ramsdale can provide foie
> grass like you're used to, but — what's that?

*Humbert has pulled a brochure from his pocket and is studying it sur-
reptitiously.*

> HUMBERT
> What? Oh . . . Timetable. Just, for when I — You know I
> think I may have to go right back to New York. This after-
> noon, actually. Baudelaire conference. You understand.

> CHARLOTTE
> *(taken aback)*
> I'm afraid you're not too favorably impressed. This is not
> a neat household, I confess. But I assure you, you will be
> very comfortable, very comfortable indeed. Now don't say
> no until you've seen the piazza. I call it the piazza.

She pushes the door open and they enter the backyard.

> CHARLOTTE
> So much work. To keep it healthy and green. A life's
> work . . .

THE PIAZZA — DAY   *Lolita in a pool of sun, half naked, turning to
look at him through dark glasses. A garden sprinkler is turning gently.
The water touches her and moves on. Her skin is wet, and where her
dress is wet it sticks to her. A black kerchief is tied around her chest.
Her hair is chestnut.*

Everything stops. There is a roaring in Humbert's ears.

*Her honey-hued shoulders. Her supple bare back. Her stomach. Her
dark glasses.*

Lolita

CHARLOTTE

That's my Lo — Dolores, my daughter. And these are my lilies.

HUMBERT
(shaken to his core)
Yes. Yes. They are beautiful, beautiful.
(pause)
Uh, how much was the room?

THE BACK PORCH — DAY   *Lolita taking clothes off a clothesline. Humbert — casually dressed, shoes off — is watching her. It is obvious he has moved in. Lolita puts the clothes in a tub, lazily brings the tub to the porch, glances at him.*

LOLITA

Hi.

Sitting on the step of the porch, she scoops peaches out of a can with her hand, and eats them. The syrup drips.

> HUMBERT
>
> You like peaches.

> LOLITA
>
> Who doesn't? You want one?

> HUMBERT
>
> No, no. I generally wait till after the sun goes down.

> LOLITA
>
> For what?

> HUMBERT
>
> Peaches.

He gazes at her bare arms. She begins to pick up pebbles with her

feet and tosses them at the can. The sound of pebbles hitting the can: ping ping . . .

                    LOLITA
    How come?

                    HUMBERT
    Keeps the lions away. I learned that in Africa.

                    LOLITA
    Learned what?

                    HUMBERT
    About peaches.

She looks at him and grins.

                    LOLITA
    You're nuts.

He gazes at the silky shimmer above her temple grading into her hair. Her feet pick up more pebbles: ping, ping. Suddenly Charlotte rises into view. She has a camera.

> CHARLOTTE
> Don't move. Don't change anything. Oh, Humbert, really!
> You look like the cat who swallowed the *canard*.

A snapshot of Humbert looking sheepish.

HUMBERT'S ROOM — HOT SUMMER DAY   *Humbert at his desk, filling his fountain pen and writing in his diary. He hears girlish voices, goes to the window, and peers out.*

> HUMBERT'S VOICE
> A normal man, given a group photograph of schoolgirls
> and asked to point out the loveliest one, will not neces-
> sarily choose the nymphet among them . . .

HAZE HOUSE — HUMBERT'S VIEW   *Lolita is outside strutting around with her friend Rose. Humbert continues as the girls call to each other.*

> HUMBERT'S VOICE
> . . . You have to be an artist, a madman, full of shame and melancholy and despair, in order to recognize the little deadly demon among the others. She stands unrecognized by them — unconscious herself of her fantastic power.

> ROSE
> *(faintly, to Lolita)*
> See you later, alligator.

> LOLITA
> After a while, crocodile.

> ROSE
> *(starting to giggle)*
> Real soon, Daniel Boone.

> LOLITA
> Get fucked, Daffy Duck.

Peals of laughter.

Humbert smiles. Lolita unblouses her flannel shirt and flaps it to cool herself. She walks over and stands in the sprinkler.

Then, as Humbert watches, she goes to the laundry line, removes her flannel shirt, and hangs it up.

HUMBERT'S ROOM — NIGHT   *He is typing. He stops for a moment — he hears a flapping sound outside. He goes to the window.*

It's the flannel shirt flapping on the line.

Humbert goes back to typing. Suddenly, a voice.

LOLITA (OFFSCREEN)

You woke me up.

He turns to see her. She is standing in the doorway in oversized pajamas, rubbing her eyes. One pajama leg is trailing.

HUMBERT

Sorry. I'll stop.

He closes the typewriter case. She smiles at him and shuts his door. He stares at the door a moment, his heart racing.

He goes to the door, opens it, and looks down the hall. Lolita's door is closed. There is a sign on it: "STAY OUT!!! THIS MEANS YOU!!!"

Humbert heads downstairs toward the kitchen. He tiptoes to the kitchen entryway and stops: there is Lolita, sitting on the floor in front of the open refrigerator, which bathes her bare legs in its chilly light. She is reading a comic, humming softly to herself, and eating ice cream out of a container balanced on one of the refrigerator shelves.

Humbert stares at her, too enchanted to move or speak or even breathe.

UPSTAIRS LANDING — DAY   *Humbert in the hallway, listening to Charlotte and Lolita.*

> CHARLOTTE (OFFSCREEN)
> I don't see why I have to waste all my energy screaming at you all day long.

> LOLITA (OFFSCREEN)
> Yeah. Right. Me either.

> CHARLOTTE
> That's about enough sarcasm out of you, young lady.

Footsteps approach the stairs. Humbert ducks back into his room.

> CHARLOTTE
> *(calling up the stairs)*
> Be back in about an hour, Humbert. And don't let her go out with Rose. She's being punished.

> HUMBERT
> I'll keep watch.

Humbert sits at his desk, fiddling with his diary. Lolita meanders into his room and looks in the mirror.

Humbert hurriedly puts his diary in a drawer. Lolita presses her eyelid.

> LOLITA
> Ow.

> HUMBERT
> What's the matter?

LOLITA

Something in my eye.

HUMBERT

Let me see.

He goes to her and gently turns her to him.

HUMBERT

Keep still.

LOLITA

It's right . . . there. See? I can feel it.

HUMBERT

There it is. You know what a Swiss peasant would use
when you get something in your eye?

LOLITA

What?

HUMBERT

Tip of his tongue.

LOLITA

You gotta be kidding.

HUMBERT

Should I try?

LOLITA

Sure.

He does. It works.

LOLITA

Wow. Incredible.

HUMBERT

Now the other eye?

> LOLITA

You dope.

She sees that he is puckering, bringing his lips toward her eye. She grins sweetly at him.

> LOLITA

Okay.

He presses his mouth to her eyelid and for a moment the mood is oddly erotic. Then she laughs and whisks out of the room.

Humbert sits, dazzled.

THE PIAZZA — NIGHT   *Humbert, Charlotte, and Lolita sit outside on cushions, with Lolita squeezed between Humbert and Charlotte in a daughterly sort of way. Charlotte and Humbert are nursing half-empty wine glasses while Lolita is playing idly with a chewed-up doll, a ballerina made of wool and gauze. Lolita is wearing her retainer. She is flicking the doll to and from Humbert's lap.*

> LOLITA

I could be a dancer. That's a major option. Because I do have a natural grace. And, you know, a sort of sad beauty.

> CHARLOTTE

Sort of sad is right.

> HUMBERT
> (to Lolita)

I'd like to see you dance some time.

> CHARLOTTE

Little girls always want to be ballerinas, don't they? I know I did. But I think I was — how shall I put it? — just a tad too plump? Is that the right word?

> LOLITA

Yes.

Charlotte scowls at her and rises.

> CHARLOTTE
> I'll get more Vouvray.

She goes in the house.

> LOLITA
> *(conspiratorially)*
> Make her take us to Hourglass Lake tomorrow.

> HUMBERT
> Me?

> LOLITA
> She'll do anything you say. She's getting a thing about you.

Charlotte returns and sits with them.

                    CHARLOTTE
Whisper, whisper. What are you two so cozy about?

                    HUMBERT
                (covering for Lolita)
Did I ever tell either of you that I was once a cook at the
North Pole?

                    LOLITA
A cook?

                    HUMBERT
Well, not exactly a cook. I just opened a few cans. It was
a weather expedition — at least that's what they said it
was. But they were lying of course. They were a bunch of
spies. It was very hush-hush. But I did shoot a polar
bear.

                    CHARLOTTE
Oh no!

*The doll flicks between Humbert and Lolita in the half light. Lolita
brushes unconsciously against Humbert.*

                    HUMBERT
But I missed.

                    LOLITA
So how come you shot a polar bear? That's a lousy thing
to do.

                    HUMBERT
Well, I found him with his mouth in the ice cream mixer. I
couldn't possibly let that pass. We lived on ice cream.

                    CHARLOTTE
I thought polar bears were the South Pole.

LOLITA
(sarcastically)
Those are penguins. Mother.

HUMBERT
Quite right. There's a very big difference between penguins and polar bears — you know what it is, don't you?

Lolita grins expectantly, sidling up to Humbert.

HUMBERT
I mean, have you ever seen a penguin-skin rug?

Lolita giggles, flipping her doll. Her arm brushes his leg.

HUMBERT
Ever walk on one? Crunch. Crunch. Terrible.

Lolita giggles with abandon. She's getting punchy. She brushes against Humbert's thigh.

LOLITA
You're out of your gourd. Humpy.

CHARLOTTE
Will you stop fidgeting with that doll?

Charlotte grabs the doll and throws it into the dark.

CHARLOTTE
And now we all think that Lo should go to bed. Lo?

LOLITA
What do you mean "we," paleface?

HUMBERT
(to Lolita)
Well, as I was saying, there I was with my special white polar bear gun. To blend in, you know.

The phone rings.

LOLITA
It's for me.

She jumps up and runs into the house, slamming the door in a way that makes Charlotte wince.

CHARLOTTE
You'll forgive Lo's bad manners, I hope. Oh, now what?

We hear a pop record, "My Carmen," booming. Lolita is dancing to it in the background.

LOLITA (OFFSCREEN)
Humbert! Look! It's my own original modern dance cre-
ation.

CHARLOTTE
(yelling)
Dolores Haze! Turn that thing down!
(to Humbert)
Honestly, she's an absolute pest. Just slap her hard if
she interferes with your meditations. Know what I would
like? If you happened to still be here in the fall, would
you mind helping her with her homework? Especially
geography, mathematics, French —

HUMBERT
(far away)
Anything. Anything at all.

HUMBERT'S ROOM   *Humbert is at his desk, writing in his diary.*
Offscreen, we hear Charlotte and Lolita bickering.

HUMBERT'S VOICE
I long for some terrific disaster. Earthquake. Spectacular
explosion. Her mother instantly eliminated, along with
everybody else for miles around. Lolita in my arms.

He cocks an ear.

CHARLOTTE (OFFSCREEN)
I've told you a thousand times, I don't like finding your
hair on the soap.

LOLITA (OFFSCREEN)
It's clean hair, isn't it?

CHARLOTTE (OFFSCREEN)
It's disgusting.

Humbert hears Lolita trudging up the stairs. He gets up, opens his
door, sits back down. He listens hard, following Lolita with his ears —
the squeak of the bathroom-door hinge, the flap of the toilet roll, the
flush of the toilet, the water in the sink, the door opening. Then Lolita
is glimpsed passing his door. And back again. Finally she wanders

in, shuffling, not looking at Humbert, picking up pieces of paper, pretending disinterest.

We examine her with Humbert. She maunders over to his desk and lackadaisically tries to read his diary.

> LOLITA

I'm sleepy today.

> HUMBERT

Me too.

> LOLITA

Really? You been having trouble sleeping?

> HUMBERT

You can't imagine.

She sits down on his lap, and, as she settles herself, wriggles on his knee. Her lips are parted.

> LOLITA

Listen. Am I getting a zit?

> HUMBERT

What?

> LOLITA

Like a pimple. You know.

> HUMBERT

Oh. You look just . . . perfect to me.

> LOLITA

No, there. See it?

He looks at her, mesmerized. She looks at him looking at her. She smiles.

CHARLOTTE
(calling from downstairs)

Humbert?

Lolita leaps off Humbert's lap and rushes out of the room.

THE HALLWAY *Charlotte is coming up the stairs just in time to see Lolita scampering down the hall. She sticks her head in Humbert's room.*

CHARLOTTE
Is she keeping you up?

She looks at him quizzically.

HUMBERT
I beg your pardon?
(pause)
Oh, no. No no no.

HAZE HOUSE — DAY *Charlotte and Humbert walking toward the blue Melmoth.*

CHARLOTTE
So you can help me pick out a perfume. I just know you have a wonderful sense of these things, living in Paris and the Cote D'Azure the way you did.

HUMBERT
Well, I'm no expert. I've always followed my nose, certainly.

CHARLOTTE
Oh, don't be so British, Professor. You know everything about everything. I just want you to choose something. Choose your favorite seduction!

She laughs and gets in the car. Lolita appears at the front door.

                    LOLITA
Hey! Where do you guys think you're going? I'm coming
too.

*Across the street, a truck has deposited a wheelchair. The driver
gets in and reverses slowly, blocking the street.*

                    CHARLOTTE
Oh, this truck! What is he doing?

Lolita runs to the car.

                    CHARLOTTE
What is she doing?

Lolita gets in, crawls over Humbert, and sits between them.

                    CHARLOTTE
What are you doing?

                    LOLITA
                    (to Humbert)
Move your bottom, you.

                    CHARLOTTE
Lo!

                    LOLITA
And behold!

The truck drives away. Charlotte jerks the car forward.

                    CHARLOTTE
You would think a child would know when she's not wanted. And needs a bath!

Charlotte grinds the gears. Humbert looks down at Lolita's bare feet.

She has adhesive tape over her big toe, and her toenails show bits of cherry-red polish. Lolita slips her hand into his. He strokes it. The car drives on. Charlotte honks at traffic.

CHARLOTTE
What have I done to deserve this?

Lolita grins at Humbert and squeezes his hand.

LOLITA
(to herself)
Hum. Mum and Hum. Hum and Mum.

BATHROOM — MORNING   *Humbert is in his pajamas brushing his teeth. As he turns off the water, we hear the phone ringing. Humbert stares at himself in the mirror, opens the door, and comes onto the landing.*

LOLITA (OFFSCREEN)
It's for me!

CHARLOTTE (OFFSCREEN)
No, it isn't. Bring Mr. Humbert his breakfast.

LOLITA
Anybody seen my other sneaker?

CHARLOTTE
Dolores!

Humbert hears Lolita approaching the stairs. He slips into his room. The door opens and Lolita appears with his breakfast tray. She has one sneaker on and one off.

LOLITA
Don't tell. I ate all your bacon.

She giggles and goes. We hear her feet skipping downstairs. Humbert grins, then sneaks out onto the landing.

Charlotte is on the telephone.

CHARLOTTE
I'm so sorry to hear it . . . Probably just a 24-hour
bug . . . Exactly, and I'm sure he'd enjoy meeting you,
too — what? . . .
(smiling coyly)
. . . Oh, I know all about those rumors . . . Jean, stop . . .
I do admit it. He's a very attractive man, but that doesn't
mean . . . Oh, now . . .

The phone is hung up and we hear Charlotte near the stairs.
Humbert freezes.

CHARLOTTE (OFFSCREEN)
Dolores —

LOLITA (OFFSCREEN)
What can you do in life with just one tennis shoe?

CHARLOTTE
Dolores, that was Mrs. Farlow.

LOLITA
So?

CHARLOTTE
So Rose has a temperature and she can't go to
Hourglass Lake.

LOLITA
So?

CHARLOTTE
So you and I and Mr. Humbert aren't going, either. We'll
go next Sunday.

LOLITA
Oh yeah?

CHARLOTTE

Lo, don't give me that tone, please. Are you ready for church?

LOLITA

I'm not going to that disgusting church.

CHARLOTTE

Young lady . . .

LOLITA

No picnic, no church.

CHARLOTTE

Fine with me, miss. It's your conscience. But your room had better be spic and span by the time I get back. And wash your hair, young lady!

LOLITA

I washed it.

CHARLOTTE

When?

LOLITA

Couple of months ago.

The door slams. Humbert listens for a moment and then slips out of the room, leaving his breakfast tray on a chair by the door.

Still in his pajamas, he goes downstairs, humming nervously. We freeze on his face as he descends.

HUMBERT'S VOICE

Ladies and gentlemen of the jury! I hope you'll try to participate in the scene that's about to be played. Even now, my heart is still thumping from it. I still squirm and emit low moans of embarrassment. But bear with me, please.

HAZE HOUSE — DAY *Humbert hears Lolita in the kitchen and sits on the sofa reading a magazine, so that she'll see him when she enters. Which she soon does, holding an apple. Lolita plops herself on the sofa next to him. Her skirt balloons up and then subsides.*

She tosses her apple in the air and catches it.

> LOLITA
> What's a conscience? Whatever it is, I don't have one.

Another toss of the apple. Humbert intercepts it and hides it behind him.

> LOLITA
> *(playfully)*
> Give it back! That's my apple!

He tosses the apple from hand to hand. She snatches it, and bites into it voluptuously.

> LOLITA
> How come you won't go to church with my mom?

> HUMBERT
> I might one of these days.

> LOLITA
> You're just like me, aren't you?

> HUMBERT
> How so?

> LOLITA
> We're bad.

> HUMBERT
> Are we?

> LOLITA
> Mmm-hmm. Pretty bad. What are you reading?

She snatches the magazine out of his hand. During the next few lines, they struggle for the magazine, and he winds up with it. She lands in the corner of the sofa, and she flings her legs across his lap.

> HUMBERT
> Thief!

> LOLITA
> Hey, what is this, something dirty?

> HUMBERT
> Dirty! It's *Look* magazine.

> LOLITA
> I hate these magazines. *Look. Life. Time.* Why do they have to have such boring names?

She snatches the magazine back and leafs through it, noshing her apple. He leans close to her. Her hair touches his temple. Her arm brushes his cheek as she wipes her lips on her wrist.

> HUMBERT
> Because they're American magazines and Americans don't like to read anything complicated.

She shifts on his lap.

> HUMBERT
> Um. Now, Americans, Lolita . . .

> LOLITA
> What'd you call me?

> HUMBERT
> Lolita. Do you mind?

> LOLITA
> I don't know. I guess not.

She turns the pages, brushing against him with her arm, her shoulder, her knee.

LOLITA
Jeez, look at this Salvador Dali guy. What a creep. How does he get his moustache like that?

Her bare knees knock together impatiently.

HUMBERT
He takes a pinch of wax, and he twists and smoothes it around his moustache, like this.

Humbert demonstrates on his own imaginary moustache. As he does, he twists toward her, under her legs.

LOLITA
Does he think that's cool?

HUMBERT
Now, as I was telling you about these Americans, if you categorize something for them —

He moves under her. Her legs twitch.

— sorry — if you just categorize what they're looking at as Life or Time when, well, it's just a lot of photographs of famous people, that's all. They might make more money if they went ahead and called it People —

LOLITA
What are you doing? Wow, William Holden! . . .

HUMBERT
I'm sorry, it's an itch — must be the fan in my room, it . . .

LOLITA
Look at him! This guy is like a dream come true. Hey! Look! I love this guy!

HUMBERT

. . . dries the air, I suppose.

LOLITA

He does that great song. You know.
(singing)
Oh my Carmen, my little Carmen . . .

Her legs twitch on his lap as she sings, and we see her bare knees knocking against each other. He begins to sing with her, off-key, making up nonsense words that she corrects, and all the while he is moving under her legs. He is breathing more rapidly.

HUMBERT

Charmin' Carmen. Started garglin'.

LOLITA

I remember those sultry nights.

HUMBERT

Those pre-Raphaelites.

LOLITA

No, come on. And the stars and the cars and the bars
and the barmen.

He moves under her. Her legs twitch. Her slipper falls off.

She rubs her heel against a pile of old magazines. Humbert's hand comes to rest lightly on her shins.

HUMBERT

The bars that sparkled and the cars that parkled . . .

She strains to put her apple core in an ashtray. As she does, her legs and buttocks shift and twist in his lap.

His eyes. Lolita's face, blurred. The sun through the curtains.

HUMBERT
. . . and the curs that barkled and the birds that larkled.

LOLITA
And oh my charmin, our dreadful fights.

Lolita almost throws away the apple core but instead brings it back to her mouth and nibbles at it.

HUMBERT
Such dreadful blights.

LOLITA
And the something town where arm in . . .

His hand goes up her leg onto her knee, and then her thigh.

HUMBERT
(breathless)
Oh, look what you've done to your thigh!

LOLITA
. . . arm, we went, and our final row, and the gun I killed you with, O my Carmen . . .

HUMBERT
Ah!

LOLITA
. . . the gun I am holding now.

Humbert massages her thigh.

HUMBERT
You've bruised your thigh!

LOLITA
(in a shrill voice)
It's nothing at all!

She wriggles and squirms, throws her head back.

HUMBERT
Ah!

He kisses her bare neck. We see Lolita's eyes.

HUMBERT
Ah, God.

LOLITA
I'll get it!

She leaps from the sofa and runs to the phone, which has been ring-ing faintly for a few seconds now. Humbert lets his head fall back on the sofa. He rouses himself, looks down at his pajamas, and glances toward Lolita on the phone. Lolita nods at him and makes a kind of yakety-yak gesture with her free hand. Her cheeks are flushed, and her hair is mussed. Her dress and bobby-sox are askew.

LOLITA
. . . yeah, but why would I ever in my whole life want to have lunch with you and Mrs. Chatfield? . . . So what if Phyllis is there? . . . Well, what's the surprise? . . . Tell me now . . . no, now . . . . Now . . . Cripes, all right, I'll come . . . No, you have to come get me . . . I don't want to walk. Bring the car — my little Carmen.

She winks at Humbert in a surprisingly provocative way. Now he tries to get up, but he and his clothes are in some disarray. Just as he begins to sneak off the sofa . . .

LOLITA
Okay. Fifteen minutes. I will change my clothes. Okay.

She hangs up the phone. Humbert, partly out of his chair, and clutch-ing his pajama bottoms around him, half-moves toward the stairs, then hesitates as Lolita approaches.

LOLITA
What's with you?

HUMBERT
With me?

LOLITA
Yeah, you're all crouchy. You sick or something?

HUMBERT
Oh. Toothache.

LOLITA
Toothache?

HUMBERT
Terrible. Think I'd better just sit back down for a moment.

She regards him, a grin playing about her lips.

LOLITA
You're a pretty funny customer.

*With a flirty look, she flees upstairs to change, singing to herself.
Humbert follows her with his eyes.*

DINING ROOM — NIGHT   *Candlelight. Humbert and Charlotte at the
dining room table. Humbert is eating cold cuts and salad. Charlotte's
plate is empty.*

*She gently touches the silver cutlery on both sides of her plate, as if
touching piano keys. She looks across the table at Humbert, smiling.*

CHARLOTTE
How do you like the salad? My dressing? It's from
Gourmet magazine.

HUMBERT
Perfectly judged. You're not eating?

CHARLOTTE
No, no. I'm happy to watch you.

He eats.

CHARLOTTE
How peaceful it is when Lo isn't here. Don't you think?

HUMBERT
Where . . . in fact . . . is she?

CHARLOTTE
Don't worry. We have the whole evening to ourselves.
And I'll give you another piece of good news. She's going
to be out from underfoot for the next two months. The
Chatfields are sending Phyllis to Camp Kewattomie —
we call it Camp Q. And Lo's going, too, thank God. On
Thursday.

> HUMBERT

What?

His eyes twitch.

> CHARLOTTE

Oh, she threw a fit when I told her about it, but she'll love it once she gets there. She's been doing nothing but moaning and groaning and bothering you, and — Humbert, my God. You look terrible. Are you all right?

> HUMBERT

Toothache. Incredible toothache.

> CHARLOTTE

Well, how awful. We're going to have to send you straight to Dr. Quilty in the morning.

> HUMBERT

No, that's all right. I'm sure a good night's sleep —

> CHARLOTTE

Well, don't be silly, you poor sweet man. Sleep doesn't cure teeth. Now, shall we take those candles with us and sit for a while on the piazza, or do you want to go to bed and nurse that tooth?

> HUMBERT

Um. Nurse that tooth.

LOLITA'S ROOM — DAY   *Charlotte and Lolita are packing for camp. Charlotte has a roll of name tags that she is cutting up: "Dolores Haze Dolores Haze Dolores Haze," etc.*

> CHARLOTTE

And I want these name tags sewn on all your things by morning.

                                LOLITA

I don't want to go.

                             CHARLOTTE

I don't believe I asked your opinion.

                                  LOLITA

I don't want to go, and you can't make me.

                             CHARLOTTE

Look. We all think it's a good idea. Professor Humbert
thinks it's a good idea, I think it's a good idea. You Are
Going!

*Lolita storms out, carrying a shoetree. Humbert is standing on the
landing, looking sheepish, and Lolita smashes his arm with the shoetree as she passes him.*

                                 LOLITA

Double-crosser!

She tramps down the stairs, as Humbert ruefully rubs his arm.

HUMBERT'S ROOM — DAY   *Out the window below, the car is being
packed for Lolita's departure for camp. Lolita is excited, Charlotte is
hopping, Louise is lugging stuff around. Up in his room, Humbert is
writing, but he can't help going to the window periodically to watch
the preparations.*

*He sees Charlotte climb in the car and slam the door. Lolita gets half
in, waving at Louise, and then looks up toward Humbert's window. A
moment later she is out of the car, scampering up the stairs.*

*Humbert hitches up his pajama pants, flings open the door, and
Lolita rushes into his arms. She kisses him full on the lips. He tries to
speak but cannot, and suddenly she is gone again, tripping back
down the stairs.*

Humbert throws himself toward the window, near tears, and watches the car pull away, with Charlotte at the wheel, silently bawling Lolita out, the dog chasing the car, and old Miss Opposite waving feebly but rhythmically from her veranda.

Humbert tears away from the window and stumbles into Lolita's room. He throws open her closet and plunges into a heap of her crumpled clothes, wrapping himself in them.

Presently, he becomes aware of Louise's voice calling from the stairs. Humbert pulls himself together and runs to the door. Louise looks a bit alarmed to see him emerging from Lo's room.

LOUISE

My, those stairs. Got something for you, Mr. Humbert.

She hands him an envelope.

HUMBERT

Thank you, Louise.

LOUISE
All right, Mr. Humbert. I'm going now. I'll be seeing you
tomorrow.

HUMBERT
Yes. Right.

*She clumps back down the stairs, mumbling to herself, and we hear
the front door shut. Humbert goes to his desk and opens the envelope. During the following speech, he gets up, staggers into the hall,
still reading, and continues into Lolita's room.*

CHARLOTTE'S VOICE
This is a confession: I love you. I have loved you from
the minute I saw you. I am a passionate and lonely
woman and you are the love of my life. Now, my dearest,
dearest, you have read this. Now you know. So will you
please, at once, pack and leave. Go. *Departez. Adieu.*
The situation, *cheri*, is quite simple. Of course, I know
with absolute certainty that I am nothing to you, nothing
at all. Oh, yes, you enjoy talking to me — and kidding
poor me — and you have grown fond of our friendly
house and even of Lo's noisy ways. But I am nothing to
you. Right? Right. So please destroy this letter and
go . . .

*Humbert, still reading, crawls into Lolita's bed. He looks devastated:
he thinks he has to leave. His eye twitches. We move from
Humbert's face to a ledge above the bed, with the roll of "Dolores
Haze" name tags, unwound. We continue up the wall behind the bed,
with pictures of William Holden and John Garfield and also a picture
of Clare Quilty, puffing Dromes next to the words: "World-Famous
Playwright Clare Quilty Says, "There's Nothing Like a Drome — The
Thinking Man's Smoke."*

*Then a tacked-up page from a magazine: it shows a radiant young
mother, a handsome young father, and a bright pre-adolescent
daughter.*

CHARLOTTE'S VOICE

. . . I shall return by dinner time, and you must be gone
by then. You see, *cheri*, if I found you at home, the fact of
your remaining would mean only one thing: that you want
me as much as I do you, as a lifelong mate, and that you
are ready to link up your life with mine forever and ever
and be a father to my little girl . . .

*We move in closer on the photo father's hand, which is nuzzling the
daughter's golden hair.*

*Lolita has crayoned an H.H., and an arrow pointing to the man.
Humbert tucks the sheet under his chin and smiles.*

HAZE KITCHEN — DAY   *Humbert downs a slug of gin. He gasps,
takes a couple of deep breaths, and then downs an even bigger slug
of gin.*

HAZE GARDEN — LATE AFTERNOON   *Humbert mowing the lawn,
lurching blearily, singing to himself. He keeps his eye on the street. A
car goes by. The dog from next door runs after it barking. Across the
street, Leslie, Miss Opposite's black gardener, is also mowing the
lawn. He waves. Finally, Charlotte's blue sedan appears. Humbert
disappears behind the house with the mower. He mows the back
lawn. He looks up. Charlotte is at the window looking down. She
sees him. He waves up at her, like a contented suburban husband.*

Close-up of Charlotte's face. Humbert turns off the mower.

HUMBERT'S ROOM — DAY   *Humbert is working on his book.
Charlotte appears, jumps on his lap, and kisses him. He groans
slightly under her weight, but when she looks at him, he smiles.*

CHARLOTTE

Now this is bliss. This is heaven on earth. Isn't it, Hum?

> HUMBERT

Mm.

> CHARLOTTE

You have to admit —
> *(she burps)*
— excuse me. You have to admit, it's awfully peaceful without Lo underfoot.

> HUMBERT

Awfully.

> CHARLOTTE

Darling?

> HUMBERT

Yes?

> CHARLOTTE

You're working on your book, aren't you?

> HUMBERT

Mm.

She toys with papers on his desk. She pulls on drawers.

> CHARLOTTE

Darling, I'm not clear about something. Did you postpone your teaching job, or cancel it completely?

> HUMBERT

Postpone. I can take it up any time I want.

Charlotte pulls on a drawer and finds it's locked.

> CHARLOTTE

Ooh, a secret drawer. What's in it?

> HUMBERT

Old love letters.

CHARLOTTE

Can I see?

HUMBERT

No.
(pause)
Charlotte, just let me finish this chapter, and then I'll join
you downstairs. All right?

She slides off his lap, a little huffily, but she's not quite ready to go.
She lights a cigarette. She picks a bit of tobacco from her tongue.

CHARLOTTE

Hum.

HUMBERT

Yes.

CHARLOTTE
I have a surprise for you. Since you don't have to worry
about that teaching job in the fall, we're going to
England. We'll finally have our honeymoon.

HUMBERT
(smiling pleasantly)
And I have a surprise for you, darling. We're not going to
England.

CHARLOTTE
What?

HUMBERT
I'm allergic to Europe, and that includes England. The
Old World isn't just old, darling, it's rotting. And no col-
ored ads in your magazines will make me warm to it
again.

CHARLOTTE
Well, whoever said —

HUMBERT
Listen. Even in the most harmonious of households — as
this one is — not all decisions are taken by the wife.
There are certain things that the husband is there to
decide.

CHARLOTTE
Hum, I —

HUMBERT
Now I'm not cross. I'm not cross at all. But I am one half
of this household, and I have a small but distinct voice.

She falls to her knees, shaking her head and clutching his trousers.

CHARLOTTE
Oh, Hum. I never realized. I've been such a fool. You're

my husband, my ruler, my god. Let's make love, right
away —

HUMBERT
Let me just finish this chapter. And bring me a gin and
tonic — would you mind?

She rushes from the room. He picks up a book and starts to read.

CHARLOTTE'S BEDROOM — NIGHT *Humbert and Charlotte are
making love, Charlotte on top, in ecstasy. Humbert gazes at a small
picture of Lolita by the bed.*

KITCHEN *Humbert washing some dishes, still singing.*

HUMBERT'S VOICE
Throughout most of July, I had been experimenting with
various sleeping tablets, trying them out on Charlotte,
who was a great taker of pills.

DOWNSTAIRS HALL *Humbert wiping his hands on a dish towel. He
heads upstairs.*

CHARLOTTE'S BEDROOM *Charlotte is splayed out on the bed,
wearing a fetching nightie, but out cold.*

HUMBERT'S VOICE
The last dose I had given her had knocked her out for
four hours. But that was not enough to guarantee me an
undisturbed night.

*Humbert looks at Charlotte and quietly sings "I'm in the Mood for
Love." She doesn't stir.*

We see him with an enormous flashlight, which he shines in her face.

We see him poke a finger at her thigh, then give it a little pinch.

We see him yell to her, prod her a bit harder, on her leg, at her waist, and play a radio loudly next to her ear. Over all this, we hear:

HUMBERT'S VOICE
So this time Dr. Melnick prescribed something more potent.

Secure in the knowledge that nothing will wake her, he slips off his clothes and puts on his pajamas, and then collapses into bed with a grateful sigh. He fluffs the pillow, falls back heavily, and then, quite pleased, rouses himself to give her a little goodnight kiss. Whereupon Charlotte wakes up and grabs him —

CHARLOTTE
Oh, Hum. At last.

— and he succumbs to her embrace like a drowning man.

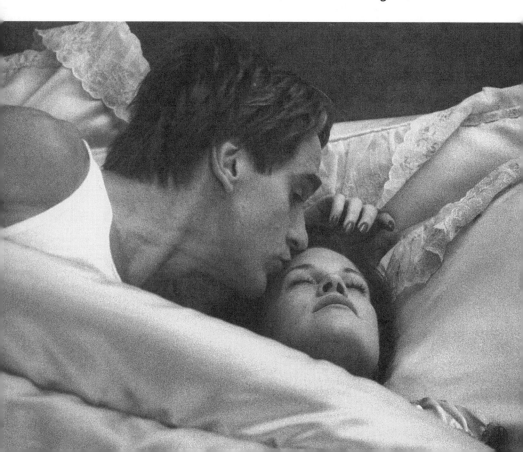

HOURGLASS LAKE — DAY   *Humbert and Charlotte park the car in a parking area and walk down toward the lake. They wear swimsuits and robes.*

> CHARLOTTE
> Do you know, Hum, I have one most ambitious dream. I would love to get hold of a real trained maid like that German girl the Talbots spoke of. And have her live in the house.

> HUMBERT
> But there's no room.

> CHARLOTTE
> Surely, *cheri*, you underestimate the possibilities of the Humbert home. We would put her in Lo's room. I intended to turn that hole into a guestroom anyway.

> HUMBERT
> Where would Lo sleep?

> CHARLOTTE
> Little Lo, I'm afraid, does not enter the picture at all. Little
> Lo goes straight from camp to a good boarding school —
> with strict discipline and some sound religious training.

*Humbert's eyes begin to twitch. He rapidly puts on his sunglasses,
and he and Charlotte walk on in tense silence.*

*They reach the lake, which is completely empty and placid, and
Charlotte spreads out a towel. She sits. Humbert stands for a
moment, and then sits beside her, fighting anger and disgust.*

> CHARLOTTE
> It's so hot, Hum. Let's go in.

HUMBERT
(*darkly*)

Yes. Let's go in.

Charlotte pulls on a black bathing cap, and they enter the water. We see Charlotte's white thighs: gooseflesh. Charlotte flings herself forward with a great splash. Humbert follows, looking intent. They swim out toward the middle.

The lake, almost empty.

Humbert watching Charlotte's head bobbing in the waves. Her pale lips. Her tight black cap. Her plump wet neck. Humbert dives. Charlotte looks around.

CHARLOTTE

Hum?

Underwater, we race toward Charlotte's flailing legs. Humbert grabs them, pulling her below the surface. She struggles and blubs.

Humbert standing on the bottom of the lake, holding Charlotte's legs. Bubbles of her last breath.

Humbert's head breaks the surface.

HUMBERT'S VOICE

But what do you know, folks. All the logic of passion had been screaming in my ear: Now is the time, now is the time. And, folks, I just couldn't do it.

We are back to him watching Charlotte's head bobbing. She has not drowned — he has only fantasized it. For one delirious moment, he thinks he has almost killed her and now must save her. He reaches out to her, and she turns in surprise.

CHARLOTTE

God, you startled me. Are you all right?

Humbert, dazed, looks at her.

> HUMBERT
>
> Sorry. I'm just — I was just following a train of thought.

> CHARLOTTE
>
> Was I on that train?

> HUMBERT
>
> You certainly were.

> CHARLOTTE
>
> You're a sweetheart.

DOCTOR'S OFFICE — DAY   *Humbert talking to Dr. Melnick.*

> HUMBERT
>
> I think I must be immune. What would you give me if I wanted to knock out, say, a cow — just for seven or eight hours? So that, you know, the cow would stay asleep even if you were tossing and turning next to it?

> MELNICK
>
> Look, try these. They're new. My wife takes 'em, and I don't hear a peep out of her all night.

> HUMBERT
>
> Sounds like just the thing.

Melnick hands him a bottle of pills.

STREET — AFTERNOON   *Humbert's car turns onto Lawn Avenue. He hums "My Carmen."*

The dog lurches after the car, barking. The car stops at the Haze house, and the dog follows it, still barking.

Humbert gets out. He raises a foot as if to kick the dog, and the dog retreats. Miss Opposite is in her chair on the verandah, rocking. She waves. A nurse in white stockings and shoes walks toward her house, depositing some letters in the mailbox on the way. Humbert picks up the newspaper the paperboy has thrown onto the porch and, with a jaunty step, enters the house.

HUMBERT

I'm home!

He stops. Charlotte is sitting at a bureau with her back to us, dressed as though for a luncheon.

She is writing a letter.

HUMBERT

Hello?

Charlotte stops writing for a moment and sits very still. Then she slowly turns in her chair.

Her face is crumpled and tear-stained. She stares at Humbert's legs.

CHARLOTTE

The Haze woman, the fat cow, the obnoxious mamma — the old stupid Haze woman is no longer your dupe —

HUMBERT

Charlotte, for heaven's sake —

Humbert sees his diary sitting on her writing desk.

CHARLOTTE

You're a monster. You're a detestable, criminal monster. If you come near me, I'll scream out the window. Get away from me!

She swings the diary at him, lunging crazily.

HUMBERT

Darling, this is all just —

CHARLOTTE
I am leaving tonight. You can keep the house — I don't
care. But you're never going to see that miserable brat
again. Get out of my sight!

Humbert staggers back, out of the room. He heads for the stairs.

HUMBERT'S ROOM *He goes in. The drawer to his table is open, the
key in the lock. He sits for a moment, thinking, his head in his hands.*

THE STAIRS *Humbert going downstairs. He walks into the dining
room and talks to Charlotte through the half-open door.*

HUMBERT
(quietly)
Listen, darling. This is nothing. The notes you found were
fragments of a novel I've been working on. Your name
and Lo's just came in handy. Part of the literary process.
Let me get you a drink. I'll show you what I mean.

Charlotte keeps writing, her back to him.

KITCHEN AND DINING ROOM *Humbert pours Scotch into two
glasses. He opens the refrigerator, which roars at him.*

*We can see that he's thinking, worried but confident that he can
change Charlotte's mind.*

*He takes out an ice tray, puts it in the sink, and turns the water on it.
The faucet whines horribly. The ice crackles.*

The icebox bangs. Humbert adds soda, which fizzes loudly.

*He carries the glasses into the dining room, on his way to the parlor
where Charlotte has been writing.*

> HUMBERT
> A little Scotch will clear both our heads — damn.

The phone is ringing. He puts the drinks down and picks it up.

> HUMBERT
> Yes?

> VOICE
> This is Leslie, sir. Across the street? Mrs. Humbert, she's
> been run over. You better come quick.

Humbert kicks open the parlor door, still holding the phone —

> HUMBERT
> There's this man on the phone saying you've been killed,
> Charlotte.

As Humbert scans the living room we see that Charlotte is not there.

*Humbert rushes out of the house. A bizarre panorama greets him.
On the far side of the street, a big black Packard has climbed Miss
Opposite's sloping front lawn. All the car doors are open.*

*We can clearly see the mailbox at the corner of Miss Opposite's
lawn. Miss Opposite is sitting in her rocking chair, staring and dazed,
mumbling to herself. Her nurse is running toward her with a tumbler
in her hand. An elderly man with a white mustache, wearing a gray
suit and a checked bow tie, is lying on the grass, his feet propped up
by a blanket. His eyes are open and he is alive, but he looks badly
shocked.*

*The dog is barking and sniffing at people. Leslie, the black gardener,
is standing with Mr. Beale, the driver of the car. Two policemen are
questioning them. Beale is shaking his head and gesticulating help-
lessly.*

On the sidewalk, under the car, a figure lies beneath a newspaper.

HUMBERT

Where's my wife?

POLICEMAN

You Mr. Humbert?

HUMBERT

I am.

BEALE

Oh, Jesus. She ran right out in front of me. I didn't have a chance.

The policeman lifts the blanket.

POLICEMAN

This Mrs. Humbert?

Charlotte's face. Her eyelashes are wet.

> HUMBERT

Oh my God. My God.

He staggers. The policeman helps him lean against the car.

> POLICEMAN

I'm very sorry, sir.

Humbert leans, dazed. A little girl in a bunny outfit touches his hand. She is holding three envelopes.

> LITTLE GIRL

She was going to the mailbox. I saw her.

> HUMBERT

Thank you.

He looks at the envelopes. The first one is addressed to Saint Quentin's Boarding School for Young Ladies; the second one is addressed to Jean Farlow, and the third to Dolores Haze, care of Camp Kewattomie. Humbert stuffs the letters in his pocket.

> HUMBERT

Officer, I've got to — I'm going to have to sit down. I'll just be over there, at home, across the street.

> POLICEMAN

You go right ahead, sir.

HAZE HOUSE — LIVING ROOM *Humbert drinking gin and burning the letters in the fireplace.*

He begins to weep. He gets up and stands in the middle of the living room. He goes to the dining room, where the two Scotches still sit. He returns to the living room.

His diary is on the floor, and he puts it in his pocket.

Slowly he goes upstairs. He stands on the landing and then enters the master bedroom. Charlotte's suitcase is on the bed, in the first stages of packing. He unpacks it and then puts it back in the closet. He stops. He looks at himself in the mirror. He goes into Lolita's room. He looks again at the page from a magazine and Lolita's crayoned H.H. He spots a bobby pin on the desk and picks it up gently.

LIVING ROOM   *An enormous vase of lilies, with a black-rimmed card that reads, "Sincerest Condolences." Pulling back, we see more lilies, more condolence cards, and Humbert, who is on the phone. There are suitcases on the floor beside him.*

> HUMBERT
> And when does she come back from her hike?

> VOICE
> Later today. Well, pretty late.

> HUMBERT
> Listen, Mrs. Holmes, I want you to handle this situation with the utmost delicacy. Dolores's mother is ill. She's been hospitalized.

> VOICE
> Why, that's just awful.

> HUMBERT
> The situation is grave, but please don't tell Dolores that.

> VOICE
> No, of course not.

> HUMBERT
> Can she be ready to leave with me tomorrow afternoon?

HUMBERT'S CAR — DRIVING — DAY

GAS STATION — EVENING   *Humbert at a pay telephone.*

> HUMBERT
> Is that the Enchanted Hunters Hotel? . . . Inn, sorry. Yes,
> this is Mr. Humbert. That's Edgar H . . . Yes, Humberg.
> No, 'bert. Bert . . . Tomorrow night. Just one night,
> please, a room with twin beds. For two. Well, one and a
> half people . . . It's just for me and my small, uh, short
> daughter.

*He goes into the gas station men's room, locks the door, and peers
at himself in the grimy mirror. From his pocket he removes a bottle of
pills, shakes a capsule into his hand, and, watching himself in the
mirror, pretends to pop one in his mouth and swallow. But the pill is
still in his hand. He tries it again, and smiles at himself in the mirror.*

CAMP KEWATTOMIE — DAY   *Humbert parks his car in a pine grove.
A red-haired boy in a green shirt is throwing horseshoes.*

HUMBERT
Hello. Can you tell me where I might find Mrs. Holmes?

The boy sullenly points.

MRS. HOLMES'S OFFICE   *Pictures of children on the walls, a framed diploma of the camp's dietitian. Mrs. Holmes, in a white camp polo shirt and black shorts, with a whistle around her neck, is sitting at her desk filling out a receipt. She rips it out of a receipt book and hands it to Humbert, who is seated across from her.*

HOLMES
And your receipt. Now she knows her mother is sick, but not how sick. She shouldn't be a minute — I just sent Charlie to get her over at the Dining Hall. She's on Decorations Committee.

HUMBERT
Charlie?

CAMP DINING HALL   *Holmes and Humbert walk toward it together.*

HOLMES
The two of them have gotten so close over the last week or so. It's such a pleasure to watch our youngsters make friends.

HUMBERT
So . . . who is this Charlie?

A sound on the steps.

HOLMES
Oh, here she is.

He turns. Lolita comes in, dragging her suitcase.

LOLITA

Hi, Dad.

He stares at her. She is very tan and very blonde, and utterly radiant.

She is wearing a tank top and wide khaki shorts, and one of her shoelaces is untied. Humbert is stunned. We go into slow motion, and there is a roaring in Humbert's ears.

Lolita smiles at him.

HUMBERT'S CAR   *Lolita sits in the front seat, chewing gum. Humbert puts her suitcase in the trunk, gets in the car, and slams the door. Lolita slaps a fly on her knee, then rolls down her window.*

LOLITA

How's Mom?

They drive.

HUMBERT

Well, the doctors don't quite know yet. It's something abdominal.

LOLITA
(perplexed)

Abominable?

HUMBERT

Abdominal.

They drive.

HUMBERT

She's in a special hospital over in Lepingville. So we'll drive to Briceland, spend the night, and then visit the hospital tomorrow. Or the next day.

LOLITA
What do you mean, the next day?

HUMBERT
Well, it's a special hospital. They may not have visiting hours every day. That's not uncommon.

She looks at him.

HUMBERT
So . . . did you have a good time at camp?

LOLITA
Uh-huh.

HUMBERT
Sorry to leave?

LOLITA
Unh-unh.

HUMBERT
Talk, Lo — don't grunt. Tell me something.

LOLITA
What thing? Dad?

HUMBERT
Any old thing.

LOLITA
Okay if I call you that?

HUMBERT
Sure.

LOLITA
So when did you fall for my mummy?

HUMBERT
Look at all those cows on the hillside.

LOLITA
I'll vomit if I see another cow.

HUMBERT
You know, I've missed you. Quite a lot.

LOLITA
Well, I didn't miss you. Fact, I've been revoltingly unfaithful to you. But so what? Cause you don't even care about me any more. Hey, you drive a lot faster than my mummy, mister!

Humbert slows down.

HUMBERT
Why do you think I don't care about you any more?

LOLITA
Well, you haven't kissed me yet, have you?

SIDE OF ROAD   *He drives off the road into the weeds. The car stops. She flows into his arms and kisses him eagerly. He is trembling, tense, not daring really to let himself go.*

A police cruiser pulls up. Humbert pushes away from Lolita. The officer rolls down his window and peers at them. Humbert straightens up, puts on a cheery smile.

HUMBERT
Hello, officer. Anything wrong?

POLICEMAN
See a blue sedan, same make as yours? They might have passed you right before the turn.

No, I don't think so.

Lolita leans across, her hand on Humbert's thigh.

LOLITA

No, officer, I didn't see any other blue sedan. But are you absolutely sure it was blue? Because we might have seen a kind of purply one, or maybe it was more red —

The police officer has already given her a friendly wave and is now driving away.

LOLITA
(giggling)

Bye-yeee

They start driving.

LOLITA

He should have nabbed you. You were doing ninety easy.

(pause)

I like that you want to go fast.

HUMBERT

You do?

LOLITA

From now on, I want everything in my whole life to go
real, real fast.

A SILENT TOWN — LATE AFTERNOON *They drive through.*

LOLITA

Wouldn't Mother be absolutely mad if she found out we
were lovers?

HUMBERT

Good Lord, Lo, don't talk that way.

LOLITA

But we are lovers, aren't we?

HUMBERT

Not that I know of. I think we are going to have some
more rain. Now, what have you been up to at camp?

LOLITA

Are you easily shocked?

HUMBERT

No. Go on.

LOLITA

Well, okay. But see, there's this one thing I can't tell you,
cause I'll blush all over.

HUMBERT

Will you tell me later?

LOLITA

If we sit in the dark and whisper, I will.

THE CAR — DRIVING — EVENING   *Through the trees, we see lights,
a bit of lake, and then the palatial Enchanted Hunters Inn. The car
pulls into a lot.*

Humbert turns off the engine.

LOLITA

Wow. Looks swanky.

*She gets out, and Humbert watches as she frees her dress from the
peach-cleft of her rear.*

HOTEL LOBBY — NIGHT   *An old black bellman wheels their bags.*
The place is full of elderly ladies and clergymen. Lolita sinks down on
her haunches to caress a cocker spaniel, which wriggles with delight.

Humbert makes his way to the front desk.

A man in a white suit — Clare Quilty — is watching Lolita with the
dog.

He sits half hidden behind a fern, and neither Humbert nor we can
quite see him.

FRONT DESK   *An elderly desk clerk is peering into the reservation*
book.

> CLERK
> I'm sorry, Mr. Humbug. I held the room with the twin beds
> till 6:30, but I didn't hear from you. We hold till 6:30 —
> that's policy. And with the flower show and the Glory of
> Christ convention —

> HUMBERT
> The name is not Humbug, it's Herbert — I mean,
> Humbert. Look, any room will do. Just put in a cot for my
> daughter. She's ten years old, poor thing, and very tired.

The clerk looks at Lolita.

LOLITA WITH DOG   *Quilty speaks from behind the fern.*

> QUILTY
> Nice dog, huh?

Lolita doesn't look up. She continues to caress the dog.

> LOLITA
> I love dogs.

We see Quilty's hands, with a distinctive ring, and we see his white suit, but not his face.

> QUILTY
>
> That's my dog. He likes you. He doesn't like everybody.

> LOLITA
>
> Who's he like?

> QUILTY
>
> He can smell when someone's sweet. He likes sweet people — nice young people. Like you.

BACK TO FRONT DESK

> CLERK
>
> I might just be able to get you into 342 — it has a double bed. Mr. Potts, do we have any cots left?

Potts turns to him. He's pink and bald and very old.

> POTTS
>
> The last cot went to 49. But our double beds are really triple. Remember last spring? We had three ladies and a child about your daughter's age, all in the one comfy bed.

> CLERK
>
> We did at that. All in the one double bed. And by all accounts, they slept wonderfully well, didn't they, Mr. Potts?

> POTTS
>
> Oh, they slept just beautifully in that big bed.

> HUMBERT
>
> We'll manage. My wife may join us later — but we'll be fine.

CLERK

Would you just sign here, Mr. Humble?

Humbert signs the register: Dr. H. Edgar Humbert and daughter, 342 Lawn Street, Ramsdale.

HOTEL ROOM   *The ancient black bellman brings Lolita and Humbert into the room. The door says 342.*

LOLITA

Hey, it's the same as our address.

HUMBERT

Mm. Home away from home.

A king-size bed with a rose chenille bedspread. Two nightlamps with frilly pink shades, and lots of mirrors.

The bellman puts down the bags and Humbert tips the bellman, who grunts and goes.

LOLITA

Wait a sec. You're telling me we're sleeping in one room? With one bed?

HUMBERT

I've asked for a cot. Which I'll sleep in if you like.

LOLITA

You're crazy.

HUMBERT

Why, my darling?

LOLITA

Because, my dahrling, when my dahrling mother finds out she'll divorce you and strangle me.

Humbert sits on the bed. Lolita studies herself in the long mirror, trying out different angles.

HUMBERT

Lo, listen a moment. I am your father. I am responsible
for your welfare. We are not rich, and while we travel, we
shall be — we shall be thrown together a good deal. Two
people sharing one room inevitably enter into a kind of —
how shall I put it — a kind of —

LOLITA

The word is incest.

*She blithely starts to explore the room. Mistaking the closet for a
bathroom, she walks into it, and then walks out giggling.*

*Then she opens the bathroom door, peers in to make sure she's
found the right place, enters the bathroom, and shuts the door.*

Humbert opens the window and takes off his jacket. He lugs the suit-

cases toward the closet, and pulls one onto the bed.

Lolita breezes out of the bathroom.

> LOLITA
> They have little things of soap.

Humbert goes to embrace and kiss her.

> LOLITA
> Look, let's cut out the kissing and get something to eat.

> HUMBERT
> I'm just rather fond of you, that's all.
> *(pause)*
> Want to see what's in that suitcase?

She stalks toward the suitcase on the bed and opens it.

> LOLITA
> Wow.

She pulls out colorful new shirts, shorts, dresses, and vests. She holds them up to herself and tries some of them on, gazing in the mirror as Humbert watches.

> HUMBERT
> You like them?

Lolita comes to him and falls into his arms. She kisses him.

> HUMBERT
> See? Kissing isn't so bad.

> LOLITA
> Only you do it the wrong way.

> HUMBERT
> What's the right way?

<pre>
                           LOLITA
         Wouldn't you like to know?
</pre>

She smiles.

HOTEL DINING ROOM — NIGHT   *There are murals of enchanted
hunters amid animals, dryads, and trees. A few scattered old ladies,
two clergymen, and, in the corner, Quilty eating alone. We still can't
make out his face.*

Lolita is finishing her main course.

<pre>
                           LOLITA
         I feel like we're grownups.

                          HUMBERT
         Me too.
</pre>

LOLITA

We get to do whatever we want. Right?

HUMBERT

Whatever we want.

LOLITA

Hey, don't look now.

HUMBERT

What?

LOLITA

That guy in the corner.

The waiter comes to the table.

HUMBERT

What guy?

WAITER

All finished, Ma'am?

HUMBERT

Yes. Thank you.

WAITER

Let me just get you cleaned up.

The waiter begins tidying up Lolita's place with a silver crumb roller. He notices her staring at it, and gives Humbert a wink.

WAITER

Now, this little roller here, it'll suck up anything. Best stay out of its way.

(pause)

Dessert?

LOLITA

I'd like the cherry pie with ice cream. And whipped cream. And extra sprinkles.

HUMBERT

"Please." And vanilla ice cream for me. Thank you.

WAITER

You're very welcome.

The waiter leaves. Humbert takes out the bottle of pills.

LOLITA

Anyway, don't you think that guy looks exactly like Quilty?

Humbert unscrews the bottle, pops a pill out into his hand, and examines it admiringly.

HUMBERT

Hm? Our fat old dentist? Back in Ramsdale?

LOLITA

Course not. His brother — The writer Quilty. Who writes the plays. You know, the smoking guy. Smokes Dromes in the ad.

Humbert, only half listening, fakes swallowing a pill, and then smiles with satisfaction.

LOLITA

Hey, what are those?

HUMBERT

Special vitamins. Want one?

LOLITA

They good?

HUMBERT

They work wonders.

LOLITA

Yeah, give me one.

She takes one. Abruptly, the waiter arrives with dessert, and Humbert quickly pockets the pill bottle.

WAITER

Who had the pie?

LOLITA

Me me me me me.

The waiter serves them.

WAITER

Hope you enjoy that.

HUMBERT

Thank you.

Lolita eats. She drops some ice cream on the tablecloth and then bends down and sucks it off with a slurping sound. Humbert watches indulgently, as we freeze —

HUMBERT'S VOICE

The pills will strike you as inexcusable, I know, but I was actually trying to preserve Lolita's purity. If she were far away, dreaming, while I held her in my arms, so that she never knew, never herself sinned —

We come out of the freeze to hear:

LOLITA

All I can say is, this stuff has camp food beat by a mile. Me and Barbara used to call it bug grub.

HUMBERT

Who's Barbara?

LOLITA

My best friend at camp. We were up —
(she yawns hugely)
— we were up at, I don't know, six this morning. Me and
Barbara —

HUMBERT

Barbara and I.

LOLITA

Me and Barbara and I went rowing at seven or so, and
then — God, I'm pooped.

ELEVATOR   *Elderly black elevator man. Lolita leans against
Humbert, holding his hand, her eyes drooping. Other passengers
looking indulgently at the sleepy little girl and her kindly dad.*

LOLITA

I was going to tell you what a bad girl —

She yawns. The women on the elevator smile.

LOLITA

— bad girl I was at camp.

ELEVATOR MAN

Past someone's bed time?

He winks. Humbert smiles nervously.

HOTEL ROOM   *They enter. Lolita sits on the bed, swaying. Humbert
kneels and, very tenderly, takes off her shoes one by one.*

LOLITA

If I tell you, if I tell you . . .

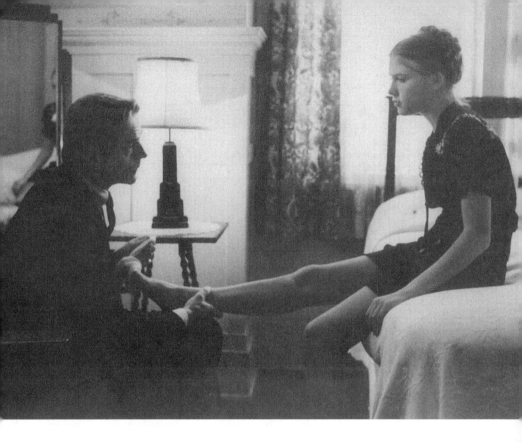

Humbert is gently taking off her socks.

> HUMBERT
> Other foot, Lo.

> LOLITA
> If I tell you how naughty I was at camp, you promise you
> won't be mad . . . ?

> HUMBERT
> Tell me later.

He stands.

> HUMBERT
> Now go to bed. I'll go downstairs for a minute, and when
> I come back I want to find you fast asleep. All right?

She removes a velvet hair ribbon and shakes her hair.

LOLITA

Oh, I've been such a disgusting girl. Lemme tell you —

HUMBERT

Tomorrow, Lo. I'm going, okay?

LOLITA

Bye, dad. 'Night.

HUMBERT

'Night.

He goes out.

HOTEL CORRIDOR   *Humbert looks at the key, and we see it close up: "342."*

He locks the door. He hangs the Do Not Disturb sign. He looks at his watch, leans against the wall, and closes his eyes. He blows a sigh of relief, and, as he walks down the hall, we see his face and hear:

HUMBERT'S VOICE
Gentlewomen of the Jury! If my happiness could have talked, it would have filled that hotel with a deafening roar. My only regret is that I did not immediately deposit key number 342 at the office and leave the town, the country, the planet that very night.

HOTEL LOBBY   *Humbert wanders aimlessly, clutching the key in his pocket. Clerics are everywhere. Humbert strolls through various public rooms, and finds himself in The Raspberry Room, which is set up for a dinner. He meanders in, goes to the window, and looks out into the gardens. The dark window reflects his face back to him, and in it he also sees, dimly . . .*

HOTEL ROOM #342   *. . . a vision of Lolita, stretched out on the bed, semi-naked in the half-light. She wears one sock; a velvet hair-ribbon is clutched in her hand. In the background, a cleric drones:*

> CLERIC (OFFSCREEN)
> To define eternity is something we will not in this room seek or endeavor to do. All we can say at this stage is that it goes on for a very, very long time indeed. And even then, you know, it has scarcely begun. So you can all see that it makes a good deal of sense to keep on the right side of the Lord.

BACK TO HUMBERT IN LOBBY

> HOSTESS
> Are you Mr. Braddock? Because if you are, Miss Beard's been looking for you.

She has crept up behind him.

> HUMBERT
> What a name for a woman.

He leaves the room quickly, but then begins drifting again. He looks at his watch and chews his thumb. The key is burning a hole in his pocket.

HOTEL MEN'S ROOM   *As the cleric continues to drone, Humbert enters the men's room and goes to a urinal. Two clergymen in clerical collars are urinating next to him, and talking to each other.*

They smile at Humbert, sweetly and condescendingly.

> CLERGYMAN ONE
> Lay brother?

Humbert looks from one to the other. They stare at him.

HUMBERT

Not exactly.

He gives himself a shake and zips up. The key jingles in his pocket.

HOTEL PORCH   *He strolls out onto the porch, which is white and columned. Bugs wheel around the lamps. Humbert sighs deeply, filling his lungs.*

We hear the rasp of a bottletop being unscrewed, and then a glug or two.

QUILTY (OFFSCREEN)

Where the devil did you get her?

HUMBERT

I beg your pardon?

Humbert peers into the darkness, but can see no one.

QUILTY

I said: the weather's getting better.

HUMBERT

Seems so.

QUILTY

Who's the lassie?

HUMBERT

Hm? Oh. She's my daughter.

QUILTY

You lie — she's not.

HUMBERT

What?

QUILTY

I said: July was hot. Where's her mother?

HUMBERT

Dead.

QUILTY

Oh. Sorry. By the way, why don't you two lunch with me tomorrow? That ghastly clerical crowd will be gone by then.

HUMBERT

We'll be gone, too. Good night.

QUILTY

Sorry. I'm pretty drunk. Good night. That child of yours needs a lot of sleep. Sleep is a rose, as the Persians say. Smoke?

HUMBERT

Not now, thanks. Goodnight.

QUILTY

Enjoy.

Quilty strikes a match to light a cigar, and Humbert tries to catch a glimpse of his face, but the light illuminates only an elderly hotel guest on a white wicker rocker.

HOTEL LOBBY   *Humbert makes his way back toward the elevators. He pushes through a constellation of clergymen and matrons. As he does, we overhear a cleric deep in conversation.*

CLERIC

George, I must tell you, when I look at the host, all I see is a wafer.

HUMBERT
(pushing through)

Excuse me.

Suddenly there is a blinding flash. Humbert has been caught in a group photograph.

HOTEL CORRIDOR   *The door to room 342. The key in Humbert's hand. It enters the lock, and, with the quietest click, the door opens.*

Humbert locks the door from the inside and turns. The door of the lighted bathroom is ajar. Through the Venetian blinds at the window, there is a glow from the exterior arc lights.

Lolita is on the bed. There are two pillows under her head. A band of pale light falls across her collarbone.

Humbert, watching, at the door.

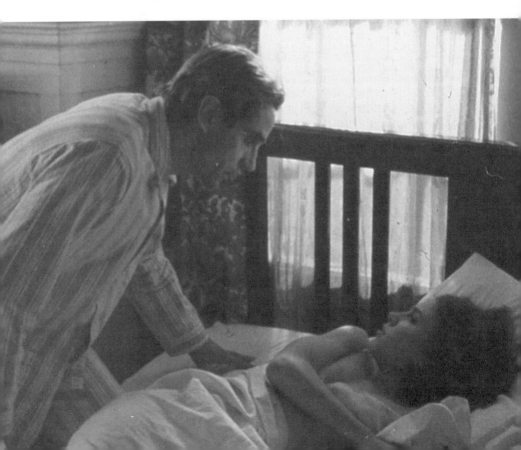

Lolita

Lolita on the bed

Humbert at the door.

Lolita on the bed.

He quickly takes off his clothes, stealthily hanging them on chairs, and slips into his pajamas. He stubs his toe on a chair. For a moment he hops on one foot, trying to restrain himself, desperate to cry out but terrified of awakening Lolita.

He calms down and limps slowly toward the bed.

His face, looking down at Lolita. He places a knee on the bed, preparing to get in. He beholds her as though she were some holy object. Lolita abruptly turns her head and stares at him through the striped shadows.

> LOLITA
> *(thickly)*

Barbara.

He freezes. She sighs, turns, and goes back to sleep. He is still, watching her, one knee on the bed. He barely dares breathe, and then suddenly his stomach growls. He grimaces dyspeptically. He stares at her to see whether she heard.

She sleeps, breathing rhythmically. Carefully, he climbs into his narrow margin of the bed and pulls over his feet the scraps of sheet that Lolita hasn't already wound herself up in. He eases himself down, watching her, but just when he reaches the most uncomfortable position, his body lying but his head still in the air, Lolita lifts her head and gapes at him. He freezes — his neck straining, his head still in the air. She looks right at him, but we can't be sure she's seeing anything.

Still frozen, he attempts a ridiculous smile.

His stomach growls.

His smile freezes, his head strains in the air. She turns back on her side and curls up. He shifts toward her, and the bed creaks loudly. Again, he freezes. He peers at her body in the moonlight. Her rumpled hair, the gleam of half a tawny haunch, half a shoulder. She breathes steadily.

His eye on her, he dares to draw nearer. But just as he begins, the elevator ascends, and the gate clatters noisily. He freezes again, in yet another impossible position. Outside, in the corridor, drunken voices laugh and yell goodnight.

Silence.

Lolita breathing. He eases toward her, very slowly. Suddenly, right next door, the loudest toilet in the universe flushes. The wall seems to shake. Humbert freezes.

Lolita, breathing.

Humbert's stomach growls, but he stops only momentarily, and begins again to near her. Someone coughs as though his lungs were coming apart. Another toilet flushes. Humbert belches.

A truck roars by. Humbert turns and looks, aghast, at the window.

Rain. The Venetian blind shifts with a little clatter, horribly magnified now. Arc lights outside. A truck roars by.

The bed. Sound of a flushing toilet. More coughing. Then silence.

Lolita breathing. Humbert moves closer to her. Her shoulder glows in the pale light.

Humbert above it. Suddenly he belches. Lolita stirs.

LOLITA
(muttering in her sleep)
You get back in the boat with Charlie, and that's that.

She tosses. Her arm strikes Humbert across the face. For a second he holds her.

LOLITA
(in her sleep)
Back in the boat.

She frees herself gently and turns her back on him and sleeps.

Humbert watches her, his head on his hand. His stomach growls. He groans quietly, gets up, and goes toward the bathroom.

He stubs the same sorry toe again, gasps, and looks back toward the bed. Lolita doesn't stir. Humbert limps toward the bathroom.

In the lighted bathroom, he pours a glass of water, drinks, pours another, drinks again. Lolita sits up.

LOLITA
I'm thirsty.

Humbert turns to her, startled.

HUMBERT
Sssh. I'll bring you something.

He fills another paper cup with tap water. He goes back into the bedroom. He sits on the side of the bed and, very tenderly, gives her the cup. She gulps down the water.

She gasps with satisfaction and hands him back the cup. Then she wipes her mouth on his shoulder and falls back on her pillow to sleep. He looks at her adoringly. He touches her arm. He withdraws his hand, lies down, and closes his eyes.

HOTEL WINDOW — DAWN   *We hear birds. A truck rumbles by.*

In the bed, Humbert and Lolita are asleep. The elevator whines. A toilet flushes.

Humbert and Lolita very close. Their eyes are closed.

His eyes open. We hear conversation in the halls. Someone says, "And a fine good morning to you!" Lolita yawns.

Humbert snaps his eyes shut, feigning sleep.

Her eyes open. She looks at him. She considers a moment and then smiles. She rolls toward him.

He opens his eyes, pretending to awaken. He looks up at her. She looks down at him, rather affectionately. She brings her head toward his. Her hair brushes his collarbone.

He caresses her hair. She kisses him, and the kiss is more romantic than he expects. Her tongue darts into his mouth. His eyes widen.

She lifts her head and examines him, as if to see whether he has had his fill and learned his lesson. He is speechless. She giggles, puts her mouth to his ear, and whispers furiously. But she breaks into laughter and can't continue.

He lies still, gazing at her. She stops laughing. She brushes her hair from her face and bends to whisper again in his ear.

                    HUMBERT
                (as she whispers)
    What game? . . . Charlie played it with you?

She pulls her head back and regards him with wonder.

                    LOLITA
    Don't tell me you never did it when you were a kid.

                    HUMBERT
    Never.

                    LOLITA
    Wow. I guess I'm going to have to show you everything.

She sits astraddle him, gazing down knowingly. Then she leans down and begins to undo his pajama bottoms. As he watches — astonished, hypnotized, mad with desire — she slowly takes out her retainer and tosses it onto the nightstand.

FADE TO BLACK

                HUMBERT'S VOICE
    Gentlewomen of the jury, I was not even her first lover.

HOTEL ROOM #342 — DAY   *We drift to the window. Gradually, the light changes from the blue-white of dawn to the yellow of mid-morning.*

A knock on the door.

                WAITER (OFFSCREEN)
    Room service.

Humbert looks at Lolita. She giggles.

> HUMBERT
> *(whispering)*
> Quick! In the bathroom.

> LOLITA
> Let's let him see.

> HUMBERT
> What?

> LOLITA
> Give him a thrill.

> HUMBERT
> Lo!

> LOLITA
> All right, all right.

She leaps out of bed, rushes to the bathroom, and closes the door. Humbert jumps up, pulls his disheveled pajamas around him, tries to rearrange the bed in a way that will look more innocent — an impossible task — and lets in the waiter.

> WAITER
> Sign here.

> HUMBERT
> Well, look at all this food. I'm ravenous in the morning.

> WAITER
> Right, right. Would you just sign here, please?

He signs.

> HUMBERT
> There you go.

The waiter leaves, and Lolita returns, giggling. They seize on the food. Lolita grabs a banana, peels it, and takes little bites from the white outer layer of it, leaving toothmarks all the way down it. The gesture is at once childish and sexy.

> HUMBERT
> Is that how you always eat bananas?

> LOLITA
> When Mom's not watching.

She gives him a long, humid look and then, very sensually and languidly, puts the tip of the banana in her mouth and slowly bites it off. He watches her for a moment, and then gently takes the rest of the banana out of her hand.

They begin once again to make love.

The view shifts to the breakfast table.

ROOM #342 — LATER   *The breakfast table, with the food mostly gone.*

Lolita is on the bed in her nightgown. Humbert is sitting in a chair wearing a robe and drinking coffee, listening raptly.

> LOLITA
> Well, so there was this girl Elizabeth? She was sort of a derelict character. So she taught me some things when we were at that other camp, but I don't really see her any more. I love that they give you potato chips with breakfast.

She grabs a few and munches.

> LOLITA
> Anyway, so in sixth grade, a lot of those kids were pretty bad. Not that bad, but — I mean, the Miranda twins used to do it on a regular basis, which I think is kind of yuck.

103

And Donald Scott did it with Hazel Smith in his uncle's garage. Dumb Donald, we used to call him — he was the dumbest boy in class. But he had the hugest, you should have seen it, he had the biggest —

HUMBERT
Let's get to the camp.

LOLITA
Well, by the time I got to camp, I knew some stuff already. And then Barbara — you know, my camp friend — and this red-haired guy, we called him Carrot-Head, but his real name was Charlie, we used to take the boat out to Willow Island, and I would be the guard while he did it with Barbara in the bushes. He's only thirteen, but I guess he'd gone a few rounds with his sister. Well, so anyway, they kept trying to get me to do it, and I didn't feel like it, but then I got so bored guarding all the time, so I did.

HUMBERT
Did? What? . . . It?

LOLITA
Yeah. Of course.

HUMBERT
And . . . how . . . was . . . it?

LOLITA
Sort of fun, I guess. Barbara says it's good for the complexion. I mean, Charlie's a big ugh — I can't stand him, but you have to start somewhere.

Humbert's face.

FRONT DESK   *Humbert paying the bill. Lolita is sitting in a blood-red armchair reading a movie magazine and following the words with her*

index finger. She wears her sundress, white bobby socks, and saddle oxfords. Her hair is neatly parted, and it shines.

Up close, we see a hickey on her neck, and a rosy rash around her swollen lips, which her tongue explores. She is wearing her retainer.

> CLERK
> Well, thank you, and I hope we'll be seeing you again real soon. Next time with the missus maybe?

> HUMBERT
> Maybe.

> CLERK
> You have a safe trip now, all right?

Humbert walks over to Lolita. She stands.

THE CAR — DRIVING — DAY   *Lolita is still reading her magazine, following the words with her finger. She clicks the retainer in her mouth. Humbert turns toward her. We freeze:*

> HUMBERT'S VOICE
> I felt more and more uncomfortable. It was something quite special, that feeling: an oppressive, hideous constraint — as if I were sitting with the small ghost of somebody I had just killed.

> HUMBERT
> *(to Lolita)*
> What are you reading?

> LOLITA
> Nothing.

He drives on.

> HUMBERT
> What's the matter?

                    LOLITA
Nothing.

                    HUMBERT
Are you angry about something?

                    LOLITA
                (still reading)
Unh-unh.

He drives.

                    HUMBERT
Lo?

                    LOLITA
Unh.

                    HUMBERT
Your friend Charlie, at camp — did he, was he the
only —

Lolita looks at him sharply.

                    LOLITA
Look, can we just get off the subject?

He drives.

                    LOLITA
Jesus.

                    HUMBERT
What?

                    LOLITA
Can we stop at a gas station?

> HUMBERT
> We can stop wherever you want.

> LOLITA
> I need a gas station. I hurt inside.

He looks at her, alarmed, but she is smiling sweetly.

> LOLITA
> Well, what do you expect? I was a daisy-fresh young girl, and you raped me. I should call the police, you dirty, dirty old man.

She giggles with pleasure at her own words. Humbert stares at her.

The car turns into a gas station and parks. Lolita jumps out and runs into the building. Humbert sits still. An elderly attendant washes the windshield with a pink sponge.

Humbert's face through the soapy windshield, staring.

He sees Lolita through the windshield as she walks toward the car.

Lolita opens the door.

> LOLITA
> I got Oreos. Give me some change. I want to call Mother in the hospital. What's the number?

> HUMBERT
> Get in. You can't call the hospital.

> LOLITA
> Why not?

> HUMBERT
> Get in and slam the door.

She gets in and slams the door.

LOLITA
Why can't I call my own mother if I want to?

HUMBERT
Because your mother is dead.

HOTEL ROOM IN LEPINGVILLE — NIGHT   *Humbert is lying alone in bed, wearing his pajamas. He is trying to get to sleep. He hears Lolita sobbing in the adjoining bedroom. His eyes open. The door swings open. She is standing there.*

Her face is swollen and crumpled with weeping. She trundles in and gets into his bed. He holds her and begins to kiss her softly and caress her hair, as we pull away from them.

HUMBERT'S VOICE
We made up very gently that night. You see, she had nowhere else to go.

THE CAR — DRIVING — DAY

> HUMBERT'S VOICE
> It was then that we began our extensive travels all over
> the United States.

Lolita wrestles with the steering wheel, trying to force a protesting Humbert off the road. They're both laughing as they struggle for control of the car, and they end up giggling like a couple of kids.

DRIVING THROUGH ARIZONA — DAY *Magnificent landscape. They pass a billboard for Coppertone — the famous ad in which the dog is pulling down the little girl's panties to reveal her tan line.*

Lolita is in the back seat reading, and her tanned bare legs are draped over the front seat. She kicks idly. Humbert is trying not to be distracted by her kicking legs, but the harder he tries the more distracting he finds them. Lolita is finishing an ice cream bar.

> LOLITA
> When's the best time to buy a bird?

> HUMBERT
> When?

> LOLITA
> When it's going "cheep."

She takes a last lick of the ice cream bar and wipes the stick across her forearm. Angle on the stick: we glimpse "When's the Best Time . . . " on one side and "When It's Going Cheep!" on the other as she wipes it. Then she throws the stick at Humbert, hitting the back of his head.

> LOLITA
> Don't say I never gave you anything.

HUMBERT
Lo, stop that!

Lolita is in the back seat, throwing things at him — more popsicle sticks, a bottle cap, a T-shirt that lands in his face and which he has to tear away in order to see the road — while he protests, "That's enough! I can't see! Not while I'm driving, Lo!" etc.

HUMBERT'S VOICE
We took a circuitous route, to put it mildly. In the back of my mind was our eventual destination, Beardsley College, where I would finally take up my teaching position.

SUNSET MOTEL — NIGHT   *The car pulls into the parking lot. Humbert opens the back door and gathers up the sleeping Lolita in his arms.*

MOTEL CABIN   *The room is dank, with yellow wallpaper and dim table lamps. Humbert lays Lolita on the bed. She murmurs drowsily. He begins to undress her, easing her out of her jacket, pulling her T-shirt up over her head. He undoes her belt, peeling off her jeans. She is wearing white socks, and, tenderly, he takes them off, one by one. As he does, we move in slowly on his face.*

He looks down at her with a kind of wonder.

HUMBERT'S VOICE
But in the front of my mind was the need to keep going, keep driving. And despite our tiffs, despite all the fuss and the faces she made and the danger and hopelessness of it all, despite all that, I was in paradise — a paradise whose skies were the color of hell-flames, but a paradise still.

Lolita

ROYALE THEATER   *Humbert is at the kiosk buying movie tickets while Lolita lurks behind him. Posters announce the feature, "Odd Man Out":*

HUMBERT
Two, please.

Stealthily, Lolita creeps up behind Humbert and, while smiling childishly at the ticket-seller, gropes him from behind.

TICKET-SELLER
One child?

HUMBERT
No! I mean yes! How much, how much —
(coughs)
— er —

TICKET-SELLER
Under twelve, it's half-price.

HUMBERT
Yes! Yes! Yes!

INSIDE THEATER   *Humbert and Lolita are moving down the aisle as a newsreel plays, and they are talking in half-whispers. The following exchange is punctuated by inserts from what's on the screen: the newsreel, the trailer for* The Bachelor and the Bobby-Soxer, *and scenes from* Odd Man Out.

HUMBERT
I'm not saying it wasn't funny — it was. But I just want to
be certain you realize . . . what could happen.

She pops her gum extra loudly, as if in reply.

HUMBERT
Look, you know I like to have fun.

He sits.

> HUMBERT
> But there are a lot of people who might look at us
> and . . . misunderstand the situation.

Lolita plops into a seat, her legs splayed, starfish-style.

> LOLITA
> *(too loudly)*
> Understand it perfectly, you mean.

*Humbert starts to speak, but shuts up as two audience members
enter the row and squeeze past them.*

> HUMBERT
> *(half-whispering)*
> Lo, there have been relationships like ours since the
> dawn of time. The Romans had them, the Greeks had
> them. The ancient Chinese —

> LOLITA
> *(much too loudly)*
> Right. I'm sure, if I called the police and told them how

you raped me, I'm sure they'd be glad to hear all about the ancient Chinese.

HUMBERT
(looking around)
Shh!
(pause)
Listen. Let's imagine you did go to the police. Let's say you told them I kidnapped and raped you. They would put me in jail, you can count on that. But what do you think they'd do with you?

Insert from the film.

HUMBERT
I can tell you what they'd do.

Another couple enters their row and squeezes past. Humbert waits, then continues.

HUMBERT
(beginning as a half-whisper but rising in intensity)
While I stood gripping the bars, you'd go to a reformatory or a juvenile detention home. Instead of me you'd have a matron weighing no less than two hundred pounds, most of it muscle and warts, guarding you with sticks and whips. And you'd have to knit things and sing hymns. Sound good? . . . Or do you think you might be better off with your old man?

She turns away from the screen and stares at him.

LOLITA
That's not funny.

HUMBERT
I know it's not funny.

LOLITA
Randy Satter went to one of those places, and they let

him out once for a week, and he was — that's not funny,
Dad.

HUMBERT

Come here, Lo.

*She leans into his arms. Reflections from the film flicker on their
faces.*

HUMBERT

You know I love you.

LOLITA

Yeah. I know you do.

THE CAR IN A DRIVE-IN RESTAURANT — DAY   *The car is dusty from
driving, and the restaurant appears deserted, despite a sign that
says "Open." Humbert and Lolita sit and wait. Humbert cranes his
neck, looking for an attendant.*

HUMBERT

It says "Open."

LOLITA

I'm hot.

*She takes off her jacket and hangs it on his head while she removes
her jumper.*

LOLITA

I want an ice-cold drink.

HUMBERT
(under the jacket)
You've been an ice-cold drink yourself lately.

LOLITA
(still undressing)
It's too hot. Let's go somewhere else.

> HUMBERT
> *(under the jacket)*
> We'll wait another minute, and then if nobody comes . . .

Lolita suddenly pulls the jacket from his head and grabs his nose hard.

> LOLITA
> I'm hungry, mister.

She glares at him for a moment and then leans over into the back seat, looking for something. Her rump is squirming next to Humbert's head.

> HUMBERT
> What are you doing?

> LOLITA
> Getting the Oreos.

> HUMBERT
> Before lunch?

Lolita turns and plops down in the seat.

> LOLITA
> Oreos are an excellent snack any time of day.

She looks at him, then grins.

> LOLITA
> I can see I'm going to have to teach you everything about how to be an American.

> HUMBERT
> Everything?

> LOLITA
> Well, I've already taught you how to kiss and all that jazz.

> HUMBERT
> And for that I thank you. Now, what else?

> LOLITA
> Okay, this is how to eat one of the major American foods.
> This is called an Oreo. And you do like this.

She breaks it in half, and slides the cream-covered side through her upper teeth until the cream is devoured and what's left on the cookie are little white toothmarks.

> LOLITA
> See? And now you do the chocolate parts.

She eats the wafers.

> HUMBERT
> And what if I want to just put the whole thing in my mouth
> and actually chew it, like a normal person who doesn't
> want to nauseate everyone in sight?

> LOLITA
> Then you would be a square and no one would ever like
> you.

> HUMBERT
> You'd like me, though. Wouldn't you?
> *(pause)*
> Lo?

The carhop finally appears. Suddenly he is thrusting two massive, snaky tubes into the car.

> HUMBERT
> What are you doing?

> CARHOP
> It's air-conditioning, see. See, the one tube gets the cold
> air to flowing in, and then the other tube, see, that takes

the hot air right out. It's real new-fangled. Now can I get your order?

Lo grabs the cold-air tube and sticks it under her shirt; the shirt billows out. Humbert stares at her, and she turns the air tube on him. Then she stuffs it down his collar, while he protests. As they giggle and cavort, the carhop can only gape.

SANDMAN MOTEL — DAY   *A fan whirring lazily from an acoustic ceiling. A stucco motel room, grimy but very large. Light is flooding in through white curtains. Near the window Humbert is sitting naked except for his pajama bottoms on a leather armchair, and Lolita, is on his lap — she is wearing nothing but his pajama tops, unbuttoned. For a moment, we cannot quite see what is going on, because Lolita is idly picking at her nose and reading the comics section of a newspaper.*

She is totally engrossed, but her hips are moving, and we gradually realize they are making love.

Insert from the comics.

Humbert's face.

Insert from the comics.

Lolita giggles, then moans. The hip movement increases.

Humbert's ecstatic face, eyes closed.

Lolita is breathing faster now, but she's back to the comics.

Insert from the comics.

A fly settles on the page. Lolita shakes it.

Humbert's face.

The fly settles on her belly, which is glistening with sweat, and wan-

ders up toward her breasts. She is breathing quickly.

Insert from the comics.

She flicks away the fly.

Humbert's face.

Lolita's face, reading the comics. She is breathing hard, and her eyes are very bright. She moans again. There seems no dividing line between her sexual pleasure and the pleasure she takes in the comics.

SANDMAN MOTEL — NIGHT *Humbert is coming out of the shower in a robe, drying his hair.*

Lolita is on the bed, lying on her side, and she has wrapped her pillow around her head so that part of it is beneath her head and part of it is on top of her head.

> HUMBERT
>
> Lo?

She doesn't hear him. Her eyes are closed.

> HUMBERT
>
> Lo?

> LOLITA
>
> Hm?

> HUMBERT
>
> What are you doing?

> LOLITA
>
> Trying to get some sleep around here.

> HUMBERT
>
> You don't usually sleep with your pillow like that.

Humbert gently pulls the pillow away, and she looks up at him, blinking.

                    LOLITA
Uh-huh I do. Sometimes. When I can't sleep 'cause the
noise is too loud. It's my sandwich.

                    HUMBERT
Is it noisy now?

                    LOLITA
There were some trucks.

                    HUMBERT
Lo, give me a minute. I'll be in bed in just a minute.

                    LOLITA
Take your time. I'm going in my sandwich.

*She pulls the pillow back around her head. Humbert looks down at
her tenderly. He quietly leaves the room.*

SANDMAN MOTEL — DAY   *Humbert closes the screen door behind
him, and pulls up a chair just outside, on the little motel sidewalk. He
sighs happily. From his pocket, he removes a photo wallet, and
examines pictures of himself with Lolita at various tourist spots: a
lighthouse, a canyon, a grotto with a sign that says, "Only Exact
Replica of Lourdes Grotto in Tri-State Area." In the pictures, Humbert
is smiling. Lolita is smiling, grimacing, and yawning. Looking at the
photos, Humbert is moved almost to tears. The camera moves to the
neon hotel sign advertising the Sandman Motel, not yet turned on.*

MOTEL — NIGHT   *The neon hotel sign crackles to life. Humbert has
fallen asleep in his chair just outside the room. Bugs whir around a
yellow light. Crickets chirp. In the distance, trucks rumble.*

Humbert awakens with a start. He hears something. Quietly, he stands up and peers through the screen door into the room. There, in the bed, still half asleep, Lolita is softly weeping.

THE CAR — DRIVING — DAY   *The countryside is now lush and green. Lolita is tossing bottle caps toward the ashtray, and mostly missing. She has something big in her mouth; it forms a lump in her cheek, and the noise she makes gnawing at it is driving Humbert crazy.*

> HUMBERT
>
> What is that?

> LOLITA
>
> What's what?

She gnaws even more noisily, just to taunt him. Humbert winces.

> HUMBERT
>
> That thing in your mouth.

> LOLITA
>
> Oh, it's a jawbreaker. Supposed to break your jaw. Want one?

> HUMBERT
>
> Just give it to me. I've had it with that noise.

He holds out his hand.

> LOLITA
>
> No! It's good!

> HUMBERT
>
> Spit it out! I have a headache!

Humbert reaches over to pull it out of her mouth. She presses her lips shut and whips her head away from him.

He grabs her by the nose, which forces her to open her mouth, and he reaches inside, grapples with tongue and teeth, seizes the jaw-breaker, and throws it out the window. Lo folds her arms and makes a face. She fishes in her shirt pocket for her retainer and pops it in her mouth.

They pass a hitchhiker.

> LOLITA
> Let's take him! Please can we? Please can we? Please?

She rubs her knees together. Humbert drives on.

> HUMBERT
> He looked like a rapist.

> LOLITA
> *(eying Humbert)*
> Oh? I didn't notice the resemblance.

She clicks her retainer at him and puts on a pair of sunglasses. She looks at him.

> LOLITA
> You look one hundred percent better when I can't see
> you.

SEA HORSE MOTEL — PARKING LOT — DAY   *Their car pulls in. A sign reads, "Children Under 14 Free."*

> HUMBERT
> To do what, I wonder?

> LOLITA
> Oh, stop it!

MOTEL ROOM   *This one is grubby stucco.*

                    LOLITA
Hey! They got Magic Fingers!

*She leaps onto the bed near the Magic Fingers slot while Humbert
undresses. She lies on her stomach with her legs in the air, so that
Humbert is effectively talking to her rear end.*

                  HUMBERT
I need a shower.

                  LOLITA

Gimme a nickel.

                  HUMBERT

What for?

LOLITA
For the Magic Fingers. Just give it to me, okay?

He reaches into the pocket of his pants, which he has just removed, and tosses a nickel on the bed.

HUMBERT
My magic fingers aren't enough?

Lolita ignores him, pops the nickel in the slot, and lies down blissfully on the bed, which begins to shake gently. Humbert starts taking his shower.

HUMBERT
(calling from the bathroom)
Good shower for once, Lo . . . First-rate temperature control.

Lolita lies still for another few seconds, and then the Magic Fingers stops. The bed is still. She gets up, goes into the bathroom, looks fiercely at the shower where Humbert is humming to himself, and flushes the toilet.

HUMBERT
Yah! My God, Lo! Don't flush when I'm in here.

LOLITA
Oh, did I flush? Sorry, Daddy. I know you hate it when I don't.

HUMBERT
Jesus!

A moment later the shower head pops off, beans Humbert, and releases an unbearable torrent of water. Muttering and rubbing his head, Humbert emerges from the shower, dries off, ties a towel around himself, and goes into the main cabin.

He's horrified to find Lolita not there, and the door wide open. Through the door, he sees Lolita by the pool. She is wearing her swimsuit and talking to a hunky teenage boy while a boy in the water stares at her bare midriff.

Humbert's face. His eye twitches.

> HUMBERT
> Lo, get in here! We're going to miss Magnolia Gardens.

> LOLITA
> *(turning back)*
> Them l'il ol' magnolias ain't goin' nowhere.

The boys laugh.

> HUMBERT
> Get in here. They close at five. And keep your feet out of that filthy pool. You could catch . . . gonorrhea.

Lolita says something saucy to the boys, and then slowly gets up and comes back into the room. She closes the door and stands in front of Humbert. She imitates his eye tic.

> LOLITA
> I'm fed up! How long are we gonna have to live in stuffy cabins doing filthy things and never behaving like ordinary people?

> HUMBERT
> Lo, you know there are limits to our financial resources. We're spending far too much on comic-books and movies and gum and jaw-splitters —

> LOLITA
> Breakers.

> HUMBERT
> You're going to have to learn to economize, young lady.

> LOLITA
> Don't say that.

HUMBERT

What?

LOLITA

Young lady. I hate that . . . She used to say that.

Lolita bursts into tears. Humbert takes her in his arms.

GAS STATION — DAY   *Lolita sucking noisily on a straw. She is in the
car while Humbert and a mechanic are looking under the hood.
Humbert hears murmurs and peers through a chink between hood
and chassis.*

*A teenage gas jockey with a cigarette in his mouth is hand-pumping
the gasoline and talking to Lolita through the car window. She is giggling.*

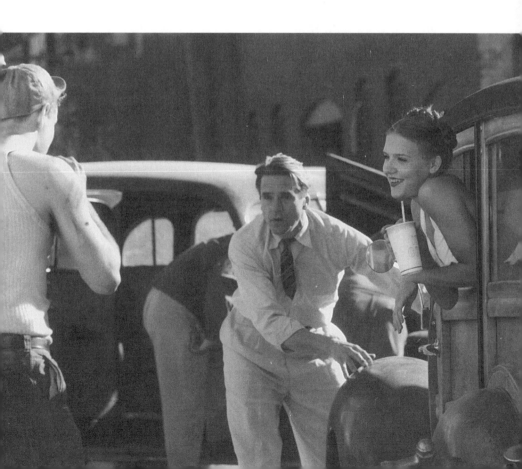

LOLITA
I'm not sure. I'd like to.

GAS JOCKEY
What I'd love, I'd sure love to take you to a drive-in. You ever been to a drive-in?

LOLITA
The thing is, I don't know if I'm gonna be here tonight.

GAS JOCKEY
Well, how else am I gonna get to know you?

LOLITA
Who says I want to know you?

She grabs the cigarette out of his mouth and takes a puff.

GAS JOCKEY
Oh, you wanna know me. I got animal attraction.

LOLITA
You act like a pig. That's a start.

The gas jockey grunts like a pig, and Humbert slams down the hood, nearly decapitating the mechanic.

THE CAR — DRIVING — NIGHT *Lolita is leaning against the far door, her legs across the seat and one foot squirming in Humbert's lap. Her other leg is stretched so that she caresses his neck and mashes his lips with her foot, even sticks her toes in his nose.*

She is also pitching bottle caps into the ashtray, and hitting it every time.

HUMBERT
. . . which makes it all very convenient. I've obviously got to make some money for us, so I'll teach at Beardsley College and you'll go to the prep school. I think you'll find

it congenial, no boys to distract you from your work. And
we'll both live a very normal —

*In a fury, Lolita draws her feet back and sits bolt upright. She squirms
into the back seat.*

LOLITA
Fat chance I'm going to go to some stuffed shirt prep
school with no boys . . .

*Now she lies on the floor, staring straight upward and kicking at the
back of Humbert's head. They speak simultaneously as Humbert
drives and Lo kicks.*

HUMBERT
. . . You'll go and you'll like it, and you'll get the fine edu-
cation that I always wanted for you. And you'll not be one
of those ridiculous vulgarians you've always hung around
with. You'll learn to write, for God's sake, you'll learn to
speak properly and sit properly and walk properly . . .

LOLITA
. . . I'd be a sap if I took your opinion seriously. What do
you know? Who asked you? Who asked you about anything? You're a stinker, and you don't know the first thing
about America or girls, or how to be a dad . . .

SIDE OF ROAD — NIGHT *A police siren sounds. Humbert pulls over
as a spotlight floods the car. Humbert rolls down the window to
receive the officer. But, in the back, Lolita can't stop raving.*

LOLITA
You can't boss me, kiddo. I despise you. Who do you
think you are? You don't even know me. You come along,
you wreck my whole life . . .

HUMBERT
Hello, officer.

Stephen Schiff

Lolita's head peeks up over the back seat, smiling sweetly.

LOLITA
Hello, officer.

COP
License and registration.

Humbert pulls them out of his wallet.

COP
You know you was going fifty in a thirty zone?

HUMBERT
I'm terribly sorry. I must have missed the sign.

The cop peers into the car. Lolita grins her sweetest grin. The cop is stern and scary.

HUMBERT
We were having a little discussion. I guess I lost track —

COP
Look, you just keep the speed down, all right? I'm serious.

HUMBERT
Yes. Fine. Thank you, officer.

The cop leaves and Humbert rolls up the window. Immediately, Lolita returns to her former fury.

LOLITA
You don't know how lucky you are, mister. I was about to tell him everything! And I should have! I hate you! Even reform school would be better than this!

Humbert's face is grim.

HUMBERT
Lo, the holiday is over.

LOLITA
(still ranting)
You can't threaten me! Who do you think you are? You're not my father! You're . . . What'd you say?

HUMBERT
I said it's over.

BEARDSLEY PREP SCHOOL — DAY

SCHOOL OFFICE   *Lots of dark wood and diplomas on the walls. Starchy Miss Pratt is perched on her desk.*

Reverend Rigger is by a bookshelf, smoking his pipe. Humbert sits across from Miss Pratt.

PRATT
Now don't get me wrong, Mr. Humbird. I know you've taken a post at Beardsley College, and I know that over there it's academics first, last, and always. Well, that's not us. At Beardsley Prep, what we stress are the three D's — Dramatics, Dance, and Dating. The Reverend Rigger is right behind us on this, aren't you, Reverend?

RIGGER
I'm with you all the way, Miss Pratt. Every inch.

PRATT
So you see. Dr. Hummer, we are not so concerned with our girls becoming bookworms or reeling off the names of European capitals or the dates of forgotten battles nobody knows or cares about anyway. For the modern pre-adolescent, medieval dates are less vital than week-end ones.

HUMBERT

Weekend whats?

PRATT

Why, dates, Mr. Humpling. Boys.

Humbert's face. He smiles wanly.

THAYER STREET HOUSE — DAY   *Humbert picks up the mail from the kitchen and enters the living room. He sits down in a rocking chair and begins to go through the mail. Lolita has put on a record. She practices dancing. Humbert watches her, and we can see that Lolita is aware that he's watching. But whenever she turns her gaze on him, he pretends to be engrossed in the mail. Finally she sits on a chair and begins painting her toenails.*

LOLITA

I'm supposed to be in a play.

HUMBERT

What play?

LOLITA

I dunno. Some play. At school.

HUMBERT

With the boys from Butler's Academy?

LOLITA

I dunno. Maybe.

HUMBERT

I don't think it's a good idea.

LOLITA

You're depriving me of my civil rights!

HUMBERT

Where did you learn that language?

> LOLITA

I'm intelligent!

Lolita dances over to him, curls down next to his chair, and begins rocking the chair with her bare foot.

> LOLITA

I have a right to be in a play if I want.

> HUMBERT
> *(being rocked)*

Not if I say you don't.

She rests her head on his knee. She puts her hand on the inside of his knee. He tries to peruse the bill he's just opened.

Her hand gently creeps a little way up his inner thigh.

He clears his throat and continues reading.

> LOLITA

You like that?

> HUMBERT

Mm.

> LOLITA

You want more, don't ya?

Humbert closes his eyes.

> LOLITA

Well, I want things, too.

> HUMBERT

What?

> LOLITA

Oh, things. You know how my allowance is a dollar a week?

Lolita

HUMBERT

I know.

She creeps her hand up his inner thigh.

LOLITA

I think it should be two dollars.

Silence. They are both still.

LOLITA

I said I think it should be two dollars.

HUMBERT

A dollar fifty.

Her hand retreats to his knee and stops.

LOLITA

I really do think it should be two dollars.

Her hand begins to creep up his thigh again.

LOLITA

Am I right?

Her hand creeping.

LOLITA

Am I right?

Her hand stops. Humbert gasps and shuts his eyes.

HUMBERT

Yes. God. Two dollars.

LOLITA

And I get to act in the play.

He is still. Her hand begins to climb up his thigh.

A HUMBERT-THE-HOMEMAKER MONTAGE:

We see him vacuuming in his apron, humming "My Carmen" as he does.

We see him doing the dishes.

We see him ironing.

We see him taking a nip of gin.

THAYER STREET — DAY   *Humbert taking in the groceries. In the courtyard, Miss LeBone, his neighbor to the east, is pruning rose-bushes. She eyes him suspiciously.*

In his apron, Humbert watches through the living room window as Lolita comes home. She is walking her bike. At her side is a boy in a red sweater who seems to be hanging on her every word.

As Humbert watches, the two stop in front of the house. They keep talking earnestly, with Lolita clutching her schoolbooks to her chest. She stands on her left instep with her right toe, then removes it backward, crosses her feet, rocks slightly, sketches a few steps, and then does the whole thing again. She feigns helpless merriment at something Red Sweater says.

Humbert is tantalized. He watches. He pours himself a drink.

BEARDSLEY PREP SCHOOL OFFICE   *Miss Pratt, again perched on her desk. Again, the Reverend Rigger standing. Again, Humbert sitting attentively.*

> MISS PRATT
> She's a lovely child, Mr. Haze, but the onset of sexual maturing seems to give her trouble. Is that your observation, Reverend Rigger?

                    RIGGER
To the tee, Miss Pratt.

                  MISS PRATT
So you see. She is still shuttling between the anal and
genital zones of development.

She makes a shuttling motion with her hand.

                  MISS PRATT
Anal. Genital. Anal. Genital.

                   HUMBERT
I beg your pardon?

                  MISS PRATT
The general impression is that fourteen-year-old Dolores
Haze remains morbidly uninterested in sexual matters.

                   HUMBERT
Has she said anything? About these . . . matters?

                  MISS PRATT
                  (ominously)
Well, that's just it.

                   HUMBERT
              (suddenly very alarmed)
What's just it? She's said something?

                  MISS PRATT
That's just it. *She* hasn't said anything.

                    RIGGER
She hasn't breathed a word.

*Humbert looks from one to the other to see whether they are toying
with him, whether Lolita has spilled the beans.*

HUMBERT
Well, who then . . . I mean, you seem to think . . .

Miss Pratt gives him a long, knowing look that terrifies him.

MISS PRATT
Exactly.
(silence)
This is a very serious matter.
(more silence)
What we are trying to say, Mr. Haze, is that someone in the family — maybe you . . .
(a long, agonizing pause)
This is very hard for me to say.

Humbert is dying.

MISS PRATT
Well, let me put it this way. Someone ought to instruct that dear child in the process of human reproduction.

In spite of himself, Humbert laughs with relief.

MISS PRATT
I see the subject embarrasses you. Yet you, as the girl's father, ought to take the matter well in hand.

HUMBERT
Oh, I have, Miss Pratt. I have taken the matter . . . well in hand.

MISS PRATT
Oh. Well, then. That's all I needed to say. I'm pleased that you've let her take those piano lessons, and I'm so glad she's participating in "The Hunted Enchanters," or what is it? — anyway, our school play. She was such a precious little nymph in the tryout, wasn't she, Reverend Rigger?

> RIGGER
Made for the role.

> MISS PRATT
Who knows, Mr. Haze? A star may be born.

He looks at her.

BEARDSLEY SCHOOL THEATER — DAY   *Mona, a sultry girl one year older than Lolita, is onstage with Lolita. Reverend Rigger looks up at them from the audience. Music plays. Humbert is watching from the wings.*

> MONA
> *(declaiming)*
Oh, rosy mistress of the night, you have enchanted many a hunter's heart. But this time, my temptress, you have met your match. For, far more than a hunter, I am a poet!

LOLITA
(declaiming)
The night has fallen, Rodrigo. The night is my realm, and not even your larking charms can penetrate its dark splendor.

REVEREND RIGGER
(rapping on the stage)
Hold it! Hold it! Mona, give us a moment. I'd like a word with Dolores.

Mona goes into the wings and stands next to Humbert. She talks to him in a stage whisper while Rigger instructs Lolita.

MONA
Hi, Mr. Humbert. Some play, huh?
(pause)
Hey, see up there? That's the actual playwright!

Humbert peers into the balcony where she's pointing. All we can see is a ringed hand, with a lit cigar glowing in the dark.

MONA
Can you believe it?

HUMBERT
Is this play any good, Mona?

MONA
Oh, yes sir — very poetical! See, Dolly's this beautiful witch and she gets to enchant these hunters, see. Reverend Rigger is really quite exercised about it.

Onstage.

RIGGER
Let the music transform you, do you see? And as it seeps into you, you'll just find you've become a witch!

                    LOLITA
You think?

                    RIGGER
Try it!
                (to the stagehands)
Music!

The music begins. Lolita starts to sway to it.

                    RIGGER
Close your eyes! Now look at you! You're a witch! Do you
feel like a witch?

                    LOLITA
        (swaying — and peeking through her closed eyes)
Kinda.

                    RIGGER
You're a witch! Aren't you? Aren't you a witch!

*Suddenly the music is very loud, Lolita is swaying to it, almost in a
trance. Mona gapes. Humbert stares.*

                    RIGGER
                (swaying with her)
You're a witch! A witch! You're a witch!

Humbert's face, his eyes wide.

BED — NIGHT   *Humbert's face, his eyes wide. He rolls over from
making love to Lolita. As he does, we see he is grasping her arm,
and her fist is clenched tight.*

*He lies back and breathes for a moment, as she strains to free her
arm from his grasp. Then he rouses himself, silently struggling with
her to open her hand. Finally she does, and an astonishing number
of coins fall out onto the bed.*

They both scramble for them, muttering, and we can see they've reached a kind of dementia, a real folie a deux.

LOLITA
Stop it! Give it back! You owe me!

HUMBERT
For that? That . . . ice-cold drink?

LOLITA
You got what you wanted.

HUMBERT
You can't do that. You can't make me pay extra right in the middle of it.

LOLITA
Oh, really? Is that against the rules? Dad?

HUMBERT
What do you need money for? You're trying to run away from me, aren't you? Aren't you?

LOLITA
Who wouldn't try to get away from you? You're old and you're creepy and you drink too much —

HUMBERT
You're a little whore!

LOLITA
And you're a bore! And you're getting FAT!

She grabs a last handful of coins and scampers out of bed, naked. He leaps up and chases her around the room. Then she flees toward her own room, with Humbert in hot pursuit. She slams the door and locks it. Humbert throws himself against the wall, spent and panting, his eyes crazed.

He goes to the mirror, pulls up his shirt, and stares wildly at his stomach in profile.

HOUSE — DAY   *Humbert is creeping around in his smoking jacket. We see everything from his jagged, half-crazed view. He peeks around corners, climbs the stairs, sneaks into Lolita's room. The rest of the scene shifts back and forth between Humbert's view and ours, as Humbert starts tearing through Lolita's things, looking for money, and looking for anything else that might inform him about her life outside his embrace.*

> HUMBERT
> *(murmuring)*
> Okay, Lo. Where's the money? Where's your little stash?

He tears through a wastebasket, looks through crumpled papers. He looks under her pillow and then hurriedly half-makes her bed. He rifles through drawers. He snatches up books and shakes them. From one thick volume, eight dollar bills flutter to the floor. He looks at the book's title, and we see it too: "Treasure Island."

> HUMBERT
> *(to himself)*
> Cute, Lo, but not cute enough.

He picks up the bills and sinks onto her bed, counting them like a madman.

KITCHEN — EARLY EVENING   *Lolita is sitting near a table reading her script, following the words with her finger. She sucks on a pencil and lolls sideways in an easy chair, with both legs over its arm. Near her is a half-eaten wedge of cherry pie and a glass of milk. Humbert is sitting nearby, preparing a lecture.*

Lolita sucks on the pencil, and jiggles her legs. Humbert tries to concentrate, but her legs are a terrible distraction.

The soft down on her legs. Humbert shifts in his chair.

Lolita's mouth, sucking the pencil. She looks over to where Humbert had been sitting. The chair is empty. She looks down. At the other end of the room, Humbert is crouching. He crawls toward her. She

watches a while, then goes back to her script. Humbert crawls to the table and bumps it to get her attention. She looks at him. He dodges, hiding his face behind the table legs. Then he peeps out and gives her a ghastly grin. She stares at him and returns to her script.

Humbert crawls under the table. She bends her head under the table to peer at him. She goes back to her script.

He crawls toward her under the table. She rolls her eyes toward the ceiling. He is under her now, looking up her skirt. He makes a low sound in his throat. Slowly, he reaches a hand up toward her legs. She shifts them away. He reaches higher.

She suddenly bends down under the table and stares into his eyes. His eye twitches. She imitates his tic.

The phone in the hall rings. He starts and bumps his head.

Rubbing his head, he goes to the phone and picks it up. He stands in the doorway between the kitchen and the hall.

HUMBERT

Yes?

VOICE

Hello, is that Mr. Humbert?

HUMBERT

Yes.

VOICE

This is Miss Cormorant . . . Dolly's piano teacher?

HUMBERT

Oh, yes.

CORMORANT

Well, it's just . . . will Dolly be attending her lesson next
Tuesday?

Lolita pulls the cherry pie toward her and takes a bite.

HUMBERT

I don't see why not.

CORMORANT

Oh, good. Because since she missed the last two — last
Tuesday and then yesterday . . .

HUMBERT

She missed?

CORMORANT

Well, I just didn't know if she was still sick, or . . .
because she didn't come.

HUMBERT

I assure you she will be there next week, Miss
Cormorant. She and I are going to have a little talk.

CORMORANT
Oh, good. Well, thank you. Bye.

HUMBERT
Goodbye.

Humbert hangs up the phone and comes back into the kitchen. Lolita is eating her pie and reading her script.

HUMBERT
How are the piano lessons going?

LOLITA
Great. Excellent.

HUMBERT
Especially since you've missed the last two. Where were you?

LOLITA
Where was I? Well, okay. I'll tell you. I should have told you before. I don't know why I didn't.

HUMBERT
You're stalling, Lolita.

LOLITA
I was in the park. Rehearsing the play. With Mona.

HUMBERT
That's your story?

LOLITA
That's what I was doing.

HUMBERT
What's Mona's phone number?

LOLITA
Mona's phone number?

HUMBERT

Come on. Out with it.

LOLITA

555-7241

Humbert strides briskly to the phone and dials.

WOMAN'S VOICE

Hello?

HUMBERT

Is Mona there, please?

WOMAN'S VOICE

Mona! It's Roy!

Humbert waits.

MONA'S VOICE

Roy, you dumb shit. I waited a half hour for you. You better have a fucking good —

HUMBERT

Mona, this is Dolores's father!

MONA

Oh. Oh, hello, sir. Pardon my French.

HUMBERT

Did you spend the last two Tuesdays with Dolores rehearsing in the park?

MONA

Let's see, let's see. The last two Tuesdays.

HUMBERT

One of them, Mona, was yesterday.

MONA

You know, Mr. Humbert, that's absolutely right. And I feel
awful bad about it. I alone am to blame, sir, believe me.
The whole rehearsing in the park thing was my idea.
Cause we didn't want to get on your nerves. Sir.

Humbert slams down the phone. Lolita is sitting very casually. She
has a white mustache from the milk.

LOLITA

Well? Did she confirm?

HUMBERT

She did. And I have no doubt that she was carefully
instructed. In fact, I have no doubt that you've told her all
about us.

Silence. Lolita wipes her milk mustache away and begins chewing on
a hangnail. She is gazing at him vacantly. Humbert can't help staring
at her legs.

HUMBERT

Lo, this must stop right away. The play, the boys, Mona
— I am ready to yank you right out of Beardsley in the
time it takes to pack a suitcase. Unless this stops —

LOLITA

Unless what stops?

Humbert kicks the stool away. Her foot falls with a thud.

LOLITA

Hey! Take it easy, mister!

HUMBERT

First of all you go upstairs.

He grabs her arm and pulls her up. She flails and fights.

LOLITA

Leave me alone! You pervert!

HUMBERT

You conniving little slut!

He slaps her. She backs away and makes a monstrous face.

LOLITA

Go ahead! You beast! You filthy foreigner! Murder me!
Murder me like you murdered my mother!

HUMBERT

Stop that! Stop it!

LOLITA

Murderer! Pervert!

He grabs her wrist and begins to pull her toward the stairs.

HUMBERT

You little whore! Planning your getaway? Is that what you
were doing?

LOLITA

Yeah, that's right, moron! Anything to get away from you!

HUMBERT

You're going to show me every penny you've been hiding, and then —

*She breaks away from him and runs out of the room. He sags into a
chair, and we hear the front door slam.*

He leaps up and heads for the living room.

*He looks out the rain-streaked window, and sees her bicycle wheels
flashing in the darkness. He runs to the front door and opens it.*

Miss LeBone, the next-door neighbor is there, looking ferocious.

LEBONE

I don't know who you people think you are, screaming
and carrying on. We do not live in a tenement here, Mr.
Humberton. This language —

HUMBERT

I do beg your pardon. It's my daughter's young friends.

LEBONE

Well, I'll thank you to —

HUMBERT

I'm sorry, I really must go.

He tears past her, running into the night.

*Humbert running up the street. He is paranoid, hysterical, crazed. A
streetcar clatters toward him, and for a moment it looks as though it
will mow him down; passengers in the white-lit interior peer out at
him.*

*At a corner, he sees a young man embracing and kissing Lolita. He
rushes toward them — but it turns out to be someone else. The rain
gets harder. Humbert is out of breath, half-running, half dragging
himself.*

*In front of a drugstore, Humbert spies Lolita's bicycle. Humbert goes
to the drugstore door. He's frantic now, but he's struggling to regain
his composure. The trouble is, he can't get the door open. He pulls,
he turns, he pushes, not hard enough, he pulls, he pushes again.
Finally the door opens.*

*He strides in. Ten paces away, in a little booth, Lolita is hunched over
the phone, talking rapidly and conspiratorially. She sees Humbert,
turns away, and hangs up just as he reaches the booth. Then she
flies out of the booth to meet him.*

                    LOLITA
Oh, good. I was just trying to reach you at home. Look,
I've made a decision.

                    HUMBERT
You have?

                    LOLITA
Yeah. So buy me a drink.

*They sit at the fountain. The pale fountain girl comes by with her
pad.*

                    LOLITA
Cherry Coke, please. With extra syrup.

                    HUMBERT
Nothing for me.

*The fountain girl puts in the ice, pours the Coke, adds the voluptuous
cherry syrup. Humbert waits in agony. Finally the drink is served, and
Lolita dives into it with gusto.*

                    HUMBERT
Tell me.

                    LOLITA
What's the rush?

                    HUMBERT
Lo.

She polishes off the cherry Coke.

                    LOLITA
Pay her, and let's blow this joint.

Humbert pays the bill, and they go to the door. Again, he can't get it open. Lolita gives him a look and opens it with ease.

Humbert walks beside Lolita as she straddles her bike, one foot scraping the darkly glistening sidewalk.

> LOLITA
>
> I want to leave school. I hate that school. I hate the play — I really do! I never, ever want to go back, ever.

> HUMBERT
>
> Don't mock me, Lolita.

> LOLITA
>
> Dad, listen. I mean this. I want us to leave, take another trip — right away! Now! Just like the last time. Only this time we'll go wherever I want to go. Okay?

> HUMBERT

Yes. Okay. Yes.

> LOLITA

Okay? I choose?

> HUMBERT
> *(dazed, near tears)*
You choose. Yes. Yes. You choose.

> LOLITA

Look, I'm getting soaked. Meet me at home, okay?

She hops on her bicycle and makes off into the night. Humbert watches her a moment and then begins to run through the rain.

THAYER STREET HOUSE   *Humbert stumbles in. Lolita is in the hall, drying her hair. She tosses her head and lets it fall.*

Humbert stares at her. He whispers.

> HUMBERT

Lolita.

She pulls off her wet sweater. Underneath, she has nothing on. She looks glorious.

> LOLITA

Carry me upstairs. I feel sort of romantic tonight.

He goes to her and sweeps her up in his arms.

THAYER STREET — DAY   *Humbert putting bags in the trunk. He closes the trunk and gets in the car, where Lolita is waiting, poring over guidebooks.*

She's marking guidebooks and maps with her lipstick.

LOLITA

So we need to be at Wace in exactly one week.

Humbert starts the car, then leans over for a look at the map.

HUMBERT

That's easily done. But why Wace in a week?

LOLITA

We gotta see the, you know, the ceremonial dances when they open Magic Cave.

HUMBERT

If you say so.

Humbert starts driving.

LOLITA

And then, exactly two weeks and four days later, we have to arrive down in Elphinstone — see?

She points. Humbert glances over.

HUMBERT

Yes.

LOLITA

And that's where we climb Red Rock.

HUMBERT

We have to climb it exactly two weeks and four days later?

LOLITA

Exactly.

She leans over and kisses him on the cheek.

LOLITA

Oh, I'm so excited.

HUMBERT

I just think it's remarkable how quickly you gave it all up.
The play especially. Weren't you just two weeks from
opening night?

LOLITA

I'm sick of that play. I hate that play and everybody
involved with it.

HUMBERT

Who wrote it again?

LOLITA

Some old woman. Clare something.

HUMBERT

A woman? I thought it was a man.

LOLITA

No. She's definitely a woman. She wears dresses. She
has a brother who's a man, but she's not a man. She's
nice, though. She liked me.

HUMBERT

She complimented you?

LOLITA

Complimented my eye. She kissed me. Right on the fore-
head. Gee, she's gonna miss me in the play. But that's
life. Right, Dad?

HUMBERT
(laughing)

Right. That's life.

LOLITA

We're bad, aren't we?

HUMBERT

Very bad.

The car rounds a corner, and as it does, it passes a police cruiser. Humbert, looking skittish, eyes the officer inside, and the officer inside stares back at him.

GAS STATION — DAY   *From far above, we see Lolita slip out of the car, calling, "Be right back." She trots to the rear of the station and out of sight, as Humbert slowly gets out of the car and talks to the mechanic. Both of them open the hood.*

Humbert's face, seen from different angles, as he nods in the heat; the gas station, with radio music coming from the open door; a red ice box; white-walled tires, motor oil; garbage cans. From across the street, a red convertible suddenly zooms away.

Lolita appears and comes across the street. She is emerging from the opposite direction from what we would have expected.

                    HUMBERT
Where have you been?

                    LOLITA
Toilet.

                    HUMBERT
The toilet's back there.

                    LOLITA
Oh. Yeah, that's true, but someone was in there. So I
went over to the . . .

*She turns and peers across the street. We dimly perceive a bar there
called Ralph's.*

                    LOLITA
. . . to Ralph's. They got restrooms there.

                    HUMBERT
Get in the car.

LAKE POINT COTTAGES — LATE AFTERNOON   *Humbert's car pulls
up to the cabin. He and Lolita get out, and Humbert starts removing
bags from the trunk.*

ROOM — SUNSET   *Humbert is eating a sandwich at a little table and
gazing at the sunset outside the window.*

*On the table is an open package of Wonder Bread, a jar of peanut
butter, a jar of jelly, paper plates and cups, and a sticky plastic knife.*

*Lolita is sitting across from Humbert. She is staring into her paper
plate. She is tearing the crusts off slices of Wonder Bread, shredding
the bread slices, then rolling the dough into little balls.*

                    HUMBERT
Now that, Lolita, is a sunset. An American sunset, worthy
of the Hudson School painters.

Lolita grunts, doesn't look up. She continues her labors.

> HUMBERT
> What are you doing?

> LOLITA
> *(sullenly)*
> This is how you're supposed to do Wonder Bread.

> HUMBERT
> You don't like the crusts?

> LOLITA
> Don't you know anything? You tear the crusts off. And you have to roll up the bread and pop it in your mouth. For a burst of flavor.

She does.

> HUMBERT
> Is that what it says on the package?

> LOLITA
> This is just stuff we know.

> HUMBERT
> Who knows?

> LOLITA
> We. Americans.

He looks at her.

LAKE POINT COTTAGES — MORNING   *Humbert is getting dressed. Lolita is still in bed.*

> HUMBERT
> Want to go explore the town?

                    LOLITA
I don't feel so hot.

                    HUMBERT
What's the matter?

                    LOLITA
I don't know. It's no big deal. Let me just stay in bed for a
while. Can you give me those comics?

Humbert brings her some comic books. He sits on the bed.

                    HUMBERT
Shall I walk down to the town and bring back some fruit?

                    LOLITA
Yeah. Bananas.

                    HUMBERT
Anything else?

LOLITA
Just bananas.

OUTSIDE CABIN   *Humbert walks off with a jaunty step. We continue to look at the window. Suddenly, Lolita appears, looking out.*

BARBER SHOP — DAY   *On the floor, among hair clippings, a brown
paper bag with bananas sticking out.*

*Humbert in a barber chair getting shaved and watching a wooden TV
with a tiny black-and-white screen. The barber stops and clicks the
channels.*

T.V. ANNOUNCER
— ilty can't be here in our Texaco Playhouse studios,
because he's in Wace, Texas tonight working on the premiere of his brand new play. But I want to welcome his

writing partner. Here she is, ladies and gentlemen, the lovely and talented Miss Vivian Darkbloom. Let's give her —

Humbert is looking quizzically at the set, but the barber clicks to another channel — Milton Berle dressed up in women's clothing.

LAKE POINT COTTAGES — DAY   *Humbert walks up the drive, carrying his grocery bag. A large girl is loaded with linen, cleaning the cabins.*

Between the cabins are garages; an elderly couple is backing out of one of them in a new car. We look down past other garages. From one, the hood of a red convertible protrudes.

A handsome young man is carrying a portable refrigerator and putting it in his station wagon. He sees Humbert and winks.

Humbert stops and looks at him, and then goes into the cabin.

As Humbert enters, Lolita is sitting on the bed, in slacks and a T-shirt, looking at him as though she can't quite place him.

At the sight of her, we go into slow motion, and there is a roaring in Humbert's ears.

Her mouth, freshly, though smudgily, lipsticked. Her hands, clasped in her lap. Humbert puts down his bag. He looks at her sandals. Then at her face. Then at her sandals again. They are filthy with gravel.

                    HUMBERT
You've been out.

                    LOLITA
I just got up.

                    HUMBERT
Don't lie to me.

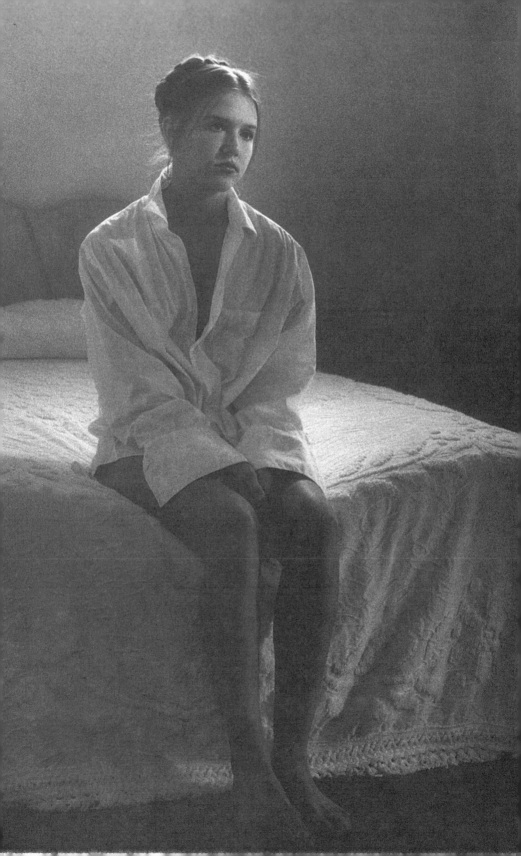

LOLITA
Oh — well, I did go out for a second, yeah. You took so
long, I went to see if you were coming back.

*Humbert goes to the window and looks out. The young man he had
spotted earlier is now loading his pregnant wife into the station
wagon. Otherwise, there is nothing much to see. He stares at Lolita.
Then suddenly he pushes her back on the bed. He stares down at
her.*

HUMBERT
Who? Who?

*With one hand, he pins her two hands above her head, and with the
other hand, he rips her shirt off. She arches against him, but he is on
top of her, sniffing at her hair and neck.*

HUMBERT
Who? Tell me who!

*He raises himself and looks down at her. For a moment, they glare at
each other. They are sweating and panting. He kisses her hard on
the mouth, and she responds hungrily, kissing back, then guiding his
arm downward. He pulls off her pants. They make love ferociously.*

ROOM — NIGHT   *Lolita is in bed, asleep. Humbert, naked, stares at
the ceiling. The sound of rain. Outside, he thinks he hears voices,
giggling.*

*He rises, goes to the window. He hears voices. He pulls back the
curtains. Nothing is there.*

*He hears a light tapping at the door. He slowly goes to the door and
opens it.*

*A man at the door is standing holding a Dick Tracy mask over his
face. In the background, shadowy figures whisper creepily.*

Humbert cries out and slams the door. Then he opens it again. No one is there. He closes the door. Again, he thinks he hears whispers and giggling in the rain.

He reels into the bathroom and turns on the fluorescent light. It is broken — it snaps and snarls and keeps blinking on and off. The sound of the rain gives way to the sound of the dripping faucet. Humbert looks into the sink, which is eerily greenish-blue in the fluorescent light. In the sink sits a cake of soap, and the dripping faucet has made a ghastly green hole in the middle of it. Humbert stares at it, and then examines his face in the mirror.

The fluorescent light blinks on, off. Humbert's face — on, off.

He stumbles out of the bathroom, and goes to his suitcase. The bathroom light continues to flicker as he burrows about in the suitcase and emerges with a folded, white woolen scarf. He opens the scarf. There is a small revolver in it. Humbert checks it.

THE CAR — DRIVING — DAY   *The red convertible in the rear-view mirror. We can see the driver in dark glasses, with a large mustache. A burst of sunlight obscures him for a moment.*

The red convertible in the mirror, only this time the driver has no sunglasses and no mustache.

Lolita is eating a banana in her usual way, toothing the white, outside part first.

> HUMBERT
> Lo, reach into the glovebox. There's a pad and pencil there.

Still holding the banana, she does.

> HUMBERT
> Okay. Write this down.

He peers into the rear-view mirror.

>   HUMBERT
>   Uh, Connecticut.

Lolita puts the banana down on the seat next to her.

>   LOLITA
>   How do you spell that?

>   HUMBERT
>   Just write Conn. C-O-N-N.

>   LOLITA
>   That it?

>   HUMBERT
>   No. Write this down. P-J-4-4-3-9-6. Got it?

>   LOLITA
>   Got it. What's the big deal?

>   HUMBERT
>   Let me see.

She shows him the pad.

>   HUMBERT
>   Put it in the glovebox. There's a detective following us.

She does, then settles back and reaches for her banana.

>   LOLITA
>   Oh, look. Your thingie.

>   HUMBERT
>   My what?

>   LOLITA
>   Your gizmo. All the nines are changing into the next thou-

sand. Oh God, when I was a kid, you know? I used to think they'd stop and go back to nines if my mother put the car in reverse.

> HUMBERT
>
> You're still a kid, Lo.

SMALL TOWN — DAY   *As they near an intersection, a traffic cop steps forward, motioning Humbert's car ahead, and then stopping the red convertible. Humbert is delighted.*

> HUMBERT
>
> Ha! See that? We gave him the slip.

> LOLITA
>
> If he's really a cop, that might not be so smart.

> HUMBERT
> *(still delighted)*
>
> I know what I'm doing. We're about to cross the state line, and he can't follow me then.

> LOLITA
> *(calmly)*
>
> Unless he's a fed.

Humbert is silent.

> LOLITA
>
> Or a fragment of your imagination.

> HUMBERT
>
> "Figment."

THE CAR — DRIVING — DAY   *Lolita is sleeping on the seat next to him, her legs curled into the fetal position, her hands together, palms facing, between her thighs. Humbert looks in the rear-view mirror. The road behind is empty.*

GAS STATION — DAY   *While the attendant is pumping, wiping the windshield, and so forth, Humbert goes into the station to buy some sunglasses. He glances out before he starts trying them on. Lolita is sitting in the car, flicking bottle caps.*

Humbert tries on some sunglasses. Then another pair. He is looking at himself in the mirror when a movement outside catches his eye.

He looks toward the car, and there he sees that Lolita is talking to someone. But he can't see who the someone is because the price sticker on the sunglasses is in the way.

Panicked, he whips off the glasses. A man in an oatmeal-colored coat is leaning on the car window and talking with Lolita, and the two of them are laughing and conversing as though they'd known each other for years.

Humbert begins to bolt toward the car, still holding the sunglasses, but, behind him, the attendant speaks.

> ATTENDANT
> You plannin' on payin' for 'em?

> HUMBERT
> What?

> ATTENDANT
> Them sunglasses. Three sixty.

> HUMBERT
> No, no. I've got to go. Here. I won't be needing these.

He hangs up the glasses again and makes for the door.

> ATTENDANT
> Well maybe you'd like to think about payin' for the gas, then.

HUMBERT

Oh. How much? How much?

ATTENDANT

That'll be six seventy-eight.

Humbert throws a wad of bills down and rushes out to the car.

Lolita is sitting calmly inside, studying a road map. Humbert gets in.

HUMBERT

What did that man say to you?

LOLITA

What man?

HUMBERT

That man.

LOLITA

Oh, you mean that guy? The guy who was talking to me?

HUMBERT

Lo.

LOLITA

He just wanted to know if I had a map. I guess he was lost.

They drive.

HUMBERT

Now listen, Lo. You're very young, and you don't know that people can take advantage of you.

LOLITA

Oh, that's very hard to imagine.

HUMBERT

Listen to me. That man is the cop who has been follow-ing us. Now I want to know exactly what you told him.

She laughs.

> LOLITA
> If he's really a cop, the worst thing we could do is show him we're scared. Then he'd know we're guilty right? Or, rather, *you're* guilty.

Humbert looks nervously in the rear-view mirror.

> HUMBERT
> Give me that pad, Lo. The one in the glovebox.

She reaches in, takes it out and hands it over. Humbert tries to look at it as he drives.

> HUMBERT
> See? It was very intelligent of us to — what have you . . . ?

Humbert drives onto the highway shoulder and screeches to a halt. We see the pad. All the numbers have been changed or erased in a way that's childishly obvious. Lolita is now gazing out the window at cows. Humbert calls her name softly. She turns to him. He hits her hard across the face. She bursts into tears.

> HUMBERT
> I'm sorry I'm sorry I'm sorry . . .

She buries her face in her hands.

WACE POST OFFICE — DAY   *Humbert collecting his mail. Lolita in the background, lounging by the wall.*

> HUMBERT
> Anything for H. Edgar Humbert or Dolores Haze?

> POSTAL WORKER
> Just checking.

Humbert idly looks over at a wanted poster. The face on it morphs into his momentarily.

> POSTAL WORKER
> Here ya go. Mr. Humbert? Your mail.

Humbert receives the letters.

> HUMBERT
> Bills. I should never have left a forwarding address.

> POSTAL WORKER
> That's what they all say.

Humbert turns to look for Lolita. She has gone.

A gnarled old man is sweeping the floor.

> HUMBERT
> Did you see a young girl? She was standing right here?

> SWEEPER
> Yup. Waved to somebody and then she left clean out of here.

Humbert goes out.

A sun-drenched Texas town. Humbert searches the street. There is no sign of Lolita. He begins to look in stores.

. . . A drugstore . . . Real Estate . . . Fashions . . . Auto Parts . . . Cafe . . . Sporting Goods.

PUBLIC GARDEN — DAY   *Humbert sits hunched on a bench.*

MAIN STREET — DAY   *Humbert is wandering in a daze. Suddenly Lolita is at his side, touching his sleeve with a timid and imbecilic smile.*

LOLITA

Hi. I was looking for you.

HUMBERT

You were looking for me?

LOLITA

Yeah. Where'd you go?

HUMBERT

Don't play that game with me. Where did you go?

LOLITA

Me? I saw a friend. A girl. From Beardsley.

HUMBERT

Who? I know the name of every girl in your group.

LOLITA

Well, see, you wouldn't know this one.

HUMBERT

Why?

LOLITA

Well, see, she was from the town. She was a townie.

HUMBERT

Good. I packed the Beardsley phone book. We'll look her up.

LOLITA

Well, but I only know her first name.

HUMBERT

Which is?

LOLITA

Dolly — like me.

HUMBERT

And what did the two Dollies do for —
                    (looks at his watch)
— forty-five minutes?

LOLITA

We went to a drugstore.

HUMBERT

What did you have?

LOLITA

Couple of Cokes.

HUMBERT

We can check that.

LOLITA

Well, she had a Coke. I had a glass of water.

HUMBERT

Good. Was it that place there?

LOLITA

Sure.

HUMBERT

Let's check.

He moves toward the drug store.

LOLITA

Come to think of it, it might have been just around the corner.

HUMBERT

Well, it's a small town. We'll have time to check them all.

LOLITA

Okay, I was just funnin' you. We didn't have a Coke. We were looking at dresses in the store windows.

HUMBERT

Which window?

LOLITA

That window.

They go to the dress shop window. A boy is vacuuming the carpet. Two mannequins are standing in the window. One is naked, wigless, and armless. The other, a tall, veiled bride, is missing an arm. On the floor lie a blonde wig and three slender arms, twisted around one another.

HUMBERT

Get in the car.

He gives her a little shove, and she trudges ahead of him toward the car.

THE CAR — DAY   *They are driving through mountains.*

Humbert's rear-view mirror: A Chevrolet Campus Cream convertible is following Humbert. In it, we can dimly make out a man with sunglasses and a mustache.

Humbert's rear-view mirror: Now a Horizon Blue sedan is following Humbert. In it we can dimly make out a man with a mustache but no sunglasses.

Humbert's rear-view mirror: Now a Surf Gray sedan is following Humbert. In it we can dimly make out a man with sunglasses but no mustache.

Suddenly, there is a loud noise, and Humbert's car begins to shudder. We hear a helpless plap plap plap.

LOLITA

You got a flat, mister.

Humbert pulls the car over near a precipice. Lolita folds her arms and puts her feet up on the dashboard.

Humbert gets out on the road to examine the flat. The other car stops fifty yards away. Humbert looks at it.

SUNGLASSES AND MUSTACHE — SEEN THROUGH THE WINDSHIELD
The pursuer is grinning and laughing.

BACK ON THE ROAD *Humbert runs toward the pursuer's sedan. It backs up a few feet. Humbert stubs his foot on a rock.*

The pursuer grinning and laughing.

Humbert looks back — and sees his own car gently creeping down-hill, with Lolita at the wheel. Humbert gallops back toward his car. He runs alongside it as it rolls.

> HUMBERT
> Lo! Pull the handbrake!

The car finally stops. Lolita looks out the window. The pursuant car does a screeching U-turn and drives away.

Humbert gets in his own car and sits hunched for a moment, breathing hard.

> HUMBERT
> For Christ's sake, what did you think you were doing?

> LOLITA
> Don't shout at me. I've got a headache.

> HUMBERT
> Lo, what's going on? Is something going on?

> LOLITA
> You should thank me. It was sliding and I stopped it.

Silence.

> LOLITA
> You should thank me.

CHAMPION HOTEL — TENNIS COURT — DAY   *Lolita's bare knee. She is raising it as she serves. She wears tennis shorts and a white halter top. Her midriff is bare and tan.*

We watch her serve to Humbert. Her movements are exquisitely graceful and pure.

She sends her first serve into the net. She mimics dismay by drooping in a ballet attitude, her hair hanging down.

A man and a woman are sitting at courtside, watching. They yell, "Hey, that's okay! Try again! Good form!" and the like.

Lolita serves again, and, as Humbert gazes at her, the ball thuds past him.

Lolita

The man and woman who were watching come onto the court.

> MAN
> Hey! Hi! Bill Mead. And this is Fay Page. Say, the little girl's got nice form. Mind if we join you for some doubles?

> HUMBERT
> No, no, I'm terribly sorry, but —

A bellboy calls from the lawn.

> BELLBOY
> Telephone for Mr. Humbert!

> HUMBERT
> For heaven's sake. Would you excuse me for a moment?

FRONT DESK   *Humbert is talking to the hotel clerk.*

CLERK
No, they hung up. But they said it was urgent. It's the —

He hands Humbert a piece of paper.

CLERK
Birdsley School. See there? Miss Pratt.

TELEPHONE BOOTH   *Humbert on the phone.*

HUMBERT
She did call me! . . . Why couldn't she? . . . Well, where
is she then? Maybe she — England? You mean right
now, today, Miss Pratt is in England?

The terror of it dawns on him.

HUMBERT
Good Lord!

He hangs up and races through the lobby, out of the hotel.

HOTEL TERRACE   *Looking down on the tennis courts. Lolita is playing with three people: Bill Mead, Fay Page, and a balding man with a
mustache and sunglasses. It is Quilty, and he is in an antic mood.*

*He dances around the court, yelling witticisms we can't quite hear,
and everyone breaks into laughter. He hits Lolita on the rear with his
racket. Suddenly, he sees Humbert descending upon him, and he
drops his racket and begins flapping his arms like a chicken. Then he
disappears into the shrubbery. Just beyond the court, we see him get
into a gray car and drive away. Humbert gallops down to the court.*

HUMBERT
Who was that person?

BILL MEAD
I have no idea.

FAY PAGE
He just busted right in on us, said we couldn't play dou-
bles without a fourth. But we never saw him before in our
lives, did we, Dolly?

LOLITA
Can we just get on with the game?

Mead and Page are having trouble controlling their mirth.

MEAD
Anyway, we gotta go. It's been swell.

PAGE
It really has. Bye, Dolly.

*They disappear into the bushes and we hear them break into laugh-
ter.*

*Humbert picks up the racket that Quilty discarded. The handle is hot.
He slumps. Lolita looks at him.*

SWIMMING POOL   *Lolita diving into the pool. She swims a length
and gets out.*

*From the shade of a tree, Quilty is watching. We still do not see his
face, although we see his ring as he pulls a bough back to watch
Lolita. Humbert stares at him from across the pool. He has little bits
of toilet paper on his face where he's cut himself shaving. He looks
haggard and sallow. Quilty is wearing sunglasses and wet, black
swimming trunks, and he pulls them up very tight. He keeps grinning,
baring his teeth.*

*Lolita, in her red swimsuit, is gamboling in the grass, rather erotically,
with a dog — the same dog Lolita met at "The Enchanted Hunters."
She is throwing a red ball, letting the dog fetch it and then tussling
sensuously with him. Quilty watches.*

*Humbert watches him. Suddenly, he gasps and clutches his chest,
as if he were having a heart attack.*

>   HUMBERT
>   *(to himself)*
> Uncle Gustave.

He calls to Lolita, a little crazily.

>   HUMBERT
> That's it, Lo. It's not a cop! It's Gustave. It's my Uncle
> Gustave.

>   LOLITA
> What?

Suddenly Humbert throws up violently on the grass.

>   LOLITA
>   *(to a woman)*
> Christ. My father's having a fit.

MOUNTAIN ROAD — RAINY EVENING   *The car is weaving; the wind-shield wipers swish. Humbert is driving, looking bleary. He swigs from a silver flask.*

>   LOLITA
> You're sure?

>   HUMBERT
> I'm okay, I'm okay. You know, maybe we should go to
> Mexico, Lo. After Elphinstone. You can climb the Red
> Rock, or whatever it is, and then we head down to ol'
> Mexico. My little Carmen.

Rain. The swish of the wipers.

>   LOLITA
> Quit drinking that stuff. Your driving's making me want to
> puke.

HUMBERT

I mean, why stay? Why stay in America and get hounded
all our lives? There's no point in staying here.

The sound of windshield wipers.

LOLITA

There's no point in staying anywhere.

THE SANDS MOTEL — NIGHT   *Humbert is at the front desk with a
woman receptionist. Lolita is in an armchair, eyes closed, very pale.*

RECEPTIONIST

If you'll just sign here, I'll — say, what's the matter with
your little daughter? Is she ill?

HUMBERT

She's just fine. She's —

He turns to look at her.

HUMBERT

My God.

HOSPITAL WARD — NIGHT   *Through a window, we see Lolita in a
bed, an I.V. in her arm. In a corridor, Humbert, carrying flowers, con-
fers with Dr. Blue.*

BLUE

It's a virus. Nothing to worry about. I've had forty cases
like this in the last two weeks.

HUMBERT

So should I just take her home?

BLUE

No. We're going to just keep her here overnight, keep her
hydrated, help her sleep.

HUMBERT

I'll stay with her then.

BLUE

Can't let you do that either. Look, you go back and get some sleep. It won't help anything if you catch it too.

HUMBERT

I've already got it. I feel terrible. Maybe I should stay.

BLUE

Go. Call us in the morning. And get some rest. I'll take those.

He takes the flowers from Humbert.

HUMBERT'S CAR — RAINY NIGHT *Humbert is hunched in his car, watching the hospital through the windshield wipers, stunned by his new solitude.*

SANDS MOTEL ROOM — NIGHT *Humbert lying on the bed, shivering and drinking gin. He is having a fever dream . . .*

 . . . about Mexico, about Lolita among the bright white towns and the saguaro deserts. In his dream, she plays in a Central American tennis competition, vying with splendid young California girls, waving and beaming in her tennis whites.

THE SANDS MOTEL — MORNING *A quiet Colorado morning. Birdsong. Mist rising in the sun.*

Humbert walks unsteadily across the lawn to the lobby.

MOTEL LOBBY *Humbert on the phone listening.*

WOMAN'S VOICE

Much better. She was up bright and early, the little angel. No sign of fever. And when her Uncle Gustave came to pick her up, we signed her out.

HUMBERT

Who?

WOMAN'S VOICE

Uncle Gustave, Dolores called him. He had a sweet little dog, and he was awful nice — had a smile for everyone. And he paid the bill in cash. Oh, and they said to tell you not to worry, keep warm, and they'll be up at Grandpa's place expecting you. And then they went off in that nice big Cadillac.

Humbert sits paralyzed.

HUMBERT'S CAR — DAY *The car screeches around corners. It side-swipes a parked car as Humbert speeds toward the hospital.*

He's in a dressing gown and pajamas, his face clenched.

HOSPITAL *The car skids to a halt. Humbert gets out, slams the door, and runs toward the entrance.*

HOSPITAL LOBBY *Dr. Blue walking with a clipboard, checking a chart. Humbert crashes through the hospital's glass front doors. Through the wardroom window, he sees a middle-aged man in the bed where Lolita had been. He charges at Blue, seizing him by the throat.*

HUMBERT

What have you done with her? Where is she? Where is she?

He pushes Blue to the floor and pounces on top of him, banging Blue's head against the ground.

> HUMBERT
> Where? Where? Where?

Orderlies and nurses fall on Humbert, pulling him away as he flails at them.

> HUMBERT
> You bastards! You're all in on it! You fucking fiends!

In the struggle, Humbert's head hits the wall with a crack.

It knocks the wind out of him momentarily, and just as he readies himself for another attack he sees, through the glass doors of the hospital, a police car pulling up outside.

He stops struggling. The orderlies hold onto him, warily. Dr. Blue approaches gingerly, rubbing his neck.

> HUMBERT
> Look, I'm sorry. I'm very sorry. A little too much to drink — worrying about my daughter, you know. He's a good man, Uncle Gustave. Grandpa's ranch — she'll be fine there.

He's backing out of the hospital as he talks.

> HUMBERT
> We'll all be fine now.

> BLUE
> You need a little rest, that's all.

> HUMBERT
> A little rest. How right you are. Thank you. You've been — thank you.

He leaves. They watch him go.

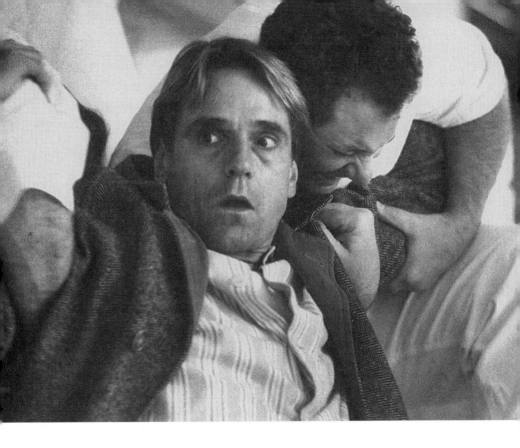

HOTEL AND MOTEL MONTAGE: *Of Humbert looking through reception books, examining signatures, murmuring things like "It won't take
but a minute."*

HUMBERT'S VOICE
I searched all our old haunts, and for several months the
trail remained warm. The thief, the kidnapper — whatever
you want to call him, he was clever. He would disguise
his name, but I could always tell his handwriting. He had
very peculiar t's, w's, and l's. It must be hard for you who
already know who it was to understand my mystification.

CHAMPION HOTEL — RECEPTION DESK   *Humbert going through
the reception book.*

LAKE POINT COTTAGES — RECEPTION DESK   *Humbert going
through the reception book.*

ENCHANTED HUNTERS INN — RECEPTION DESK   *Humbert going through the reception book. Mr. Potts and the clerk watch him curiously, and steal a glance at each other.*

DESERT — DAY   *Humbert's car stationary in the middle of the desert. Wind.*

Several different angles viewing him.

> HUMBERT'S VOICE
> Or maybe you think I was imagining things. Maybe you think it impossible that there could have been another like me, another mad lover of nymphets following us over the great and ugly plains. Well, you are right, of course. There was no one else like me.

THAYER STREET HOUSE — DAY   *Humbert in front of the house, cleaning up the car and throwing what he finds there in a garbage can: Lolita's old comics and movie magazines, Oreo and Wonder Bread packages, banana peels.*

> HUMBERT'S VOICE
> Eventually, the trail went cold and dead. And I went back to cold, dead Beardsley.

HOUSE — NIGHT   *Humbert in Lolita's old bedroom. A suitcase is on the bed. He gently folds her shirts, jeans, dresses, and places them in the case.*

He adds a pair of old sneakers, a crumpled school cap, a pair of galoshes. He lies on the bed and stares at the ceiling.

THAYER STREET HOUSE — EMPTY COURTYARD

TITLE:

THREE YEARS LATER

LETTER SLOT IN THE FRONT DOOR   *Mail tumbles through and lands on the floor.*

Humbert in pajamas walking slowly toward the door. He seems to be much older. He picks up the mail and begins sorting through it. Mostly bills. Then he sees an envelope written in a childish, rounded hand.

We see the envelope close up. The return address is: "Mrs. Richard F. Schiller, 419 Hunter Road, Coalmont 2, New Jersey."

He walks back to the sitting room, sits down next to a table on which we can see a glass of gin, opens and reads the letter.

> LOLITA'S VOICE
> November 18, 1950. Dear Dad, How's everything? I'm married. I'm going to have a baby. I guess it'll come right around Christmas. This is a hard letter to write. I'm going nuts because we don't have enough to pay our debts and get out of here. Dick has been promised a big job in Alaska. Are you still mad at me? Please send us a check, Dad. We could manage with three or four hundred, or even less. Anything is welcome. I have gone through much sadness and hardship. Yours expecting, Dolly. (Mrs. Richard F. Schiller)

A GLADE   *On a gray day, Humbert has parked his Melmoth at the end of a dirt road. He has stretched a moth-eaten gray sweater across some branches on a bush, and now he is firing his revolver at it. As he shoots, he mutters under his breath.*

> HUMBERT
> Dick. Dick has been promised a big job. Dick has been promised a very big job.

HUNTER ROAD, COALMONT — DAY   *The blue Melmoth is creeping down a rutted road. Gray drizzle, red mud, smokestacks in the distance.*

Coalmont is a dismal town, and this is its drabbest district. The street is lined with clapboard shacks, and Humbert stops at the last one.

Humbert sits inside the car. We hear the sound of hammering behind the house. Humbert opens the glove compartment and takes out the revolver. He checks it and puts it in his pocket.

Humbert gets out of the car and slams the door. A dog emerges from behind the house and woofs at him. Humbert goes to the door and rings the bell. The dog woofs again. Humbert puts his hand in his pocket. The door opens.

Lolita is seventeen now, and frankly and hugely pregnant. She is pale and wears pink-rimmed glasses, a brown, sleeveless cotton dress, and sloppy felt slippers.

> LOLITA
>
> We-e-ell!

Humbert's hand in his pocket.

> HUMBERT
>
> Husband at home?

> LOLITA
>
> Come in.

She flattens herself to let him pass. He squeezes by her bulging belly. His teeth are chattering.

> LOLITA
> *(to the dog)*
>
> No! You stay out!

She closes the door. They are in a drab parlor-bedroom that leads down into a kitchen. The back door is open, and through it you can see a dark-haired man in overalls perched on a ladder hammering something. Next to him is a plumpish man who is missing an arm.

Humbert's face, looking out at Dick.

HUMBERT
Is that him? On the ladder?

LOLITA
You want me to call him in?

Humbert takes his hand off the revolver and sags a little.

HUMBERT
No. He's not the man I want.

They sit on the divan. Lolita looks at him sharply.

LOLITA
He's not the what?

HUMBERT
You know what I'm talking about. Where is he?

LOLITA
You're not going to bring that up.

HUMBERT
I certainly am.

LOLITA
Look, Dick has nothing to do with that stuff. He thinks you're my father. Don't bring up all that muck.

HUMBERT
Who was he? What was his name?

LOLITA
You already know his name. Why are you doing this?

>   HUMBERT
> Just tell me his name.

>   LOLITA
> Want a cigarette?

>   HUMBERT
> All right.

He makes as if to get up and leave.

>   LOLITA
> You really don't know?

Humbert stands transfixed.

>   LOLITA
> My God, Dad. It was Quilty. Clare Quilty.

Humbert falls back onto the divan. He looks at her.

>   HUMBERT
>   *(a little dazed)*
> Yes. Yes, of course.

>   LOLITA
> He wrote that play I was in? "The Enchanted Hunters"?
> He was writing it when he saw us that time. At the hotel
> or inn or whatever it was?

>   HUMBERT
> Quilty. The dentist's brother.

>   LOLITA
> Yeah. He was the only man I was ever crazy about.

>   HUMBERT
> What about Dick?

LOLITA

Oh, Dick's a lamb. I mean, we're happy and all that, but I'm talking about something different.

He looks at her.

LOLITA

You know.

HUMBERT

And what about me?

Lolita is speechless. She looks at him as though she can't believe he ever expected to be taken seriously.

Humbert's face. He is crushed, obliterated, dying.

Noise comes from the kitchen, where Dick and his friend Bill are getting themselves beers. Dick comes in, holding out his hand and giving a friendly grin.

LOLITA
(shouting)
Dick, this is my dad. Can you believe it?

Dick shakes Humbert's hand.

DICK

Gosh. Glad to meet you, sir.

The one-armed man, Bill, comes into the room, bringing in the beer cans he's opened with one hand.

LOLITA

And this is Bill. My dad.

BILL

Well, I'll be. Howdy.

HUMBERT

Um, howdy.

They all stand awkwardly for a moment.

BILL

I'll just get back to the job.

LOLITA

No, Bill, stay. Dad, you can sit over there.

Humbert sits in a rickety rocker. Lolita looks around uncomfortably and then goes out into the kitchen. She returns a second later, bearing treats.

LOLITA

We got marshmallows. And we got these potato chips.

DICK

We don't have an awful lot of space, but Dolly and I could set up a mattress in the kitchen, right, Doll? You could have the couch. Folds out into a bed, see?

HUMBERT

Oh, I'm, I'm not staying. No, thank you very much. I have to be on my way.

LOLITA
(shouting to Dick)

He has to be on his way!
(to Humbert)
Dick's a little deaf. He has to be on his way! Hey, Bill, look at you. You're bleeding.

BILL

Oh. Yeah. How about that?

LOLITA

Let me see that.

Bill's thumb has been cut, and it is dripping. Lolita grabs his hand and hustles him into the kitchen for a bandage.

For an awkward moment Dick and Humbert look at each other and then look away. Dick seems about to speak, but instead he takes a long sip of beer. More awkward silence.

> HUMBERT
> So you're going to Canada?

Dick looks puzzled. Humbert shouts.

> HUMBERT
> Alaska? I mean Alaska?

> DICK
> You'll ask her what?

> HUMBERT
> No. You — Are you going to Alaska?

> DICK
> Oh. Sorry. He cut it on a jagger, I guess. Lost his right arm in Italy.

Humbert sits dumbfounded. Fortunately, Lolita and Bill return at that moment, Bill holding his bandaged thumb triumphantly aloft.

> BILL
> Look how she done me.

Dick stands.

> DICK
> Well, I guess we got some wires to fix, don't we, Bill. You all probably got loads to talk about.

He smiles. He and Bill return to the yard. Lolita lights a cigarette, inhales, taps it toward the hearth, and picks a bit of tobacco from her tongue, just as her mother had done.

LOLITA

Sure you don't want a ciggy?

HUMBERT

Where did he take you? What did he do with you?

LOLITA

Oh God.

HUMBERT

Tell me.

LOLITA

Well, everybody knew he liked little girls. He used to film them at this mansion he had in Parkington — Pavor Manor? But he was a genius. He wasn't like you or me.

HUMBERT

He was a pig.

LOLITA

He understood me. And I needed to talk to someone. Because I felt so alone.

Humbert stares at her. He is crumbling inside.

LOLITA

See, he wasn't like you. He just wanted to have fun all the time.

HUMBERT

Where did he take you?

LOLITA

Oh, he said he was going to take me to Hollywood to arrange some big audition, but we never got there. We went to this dude ranch, which was pretty amazing — I mean, they had an indoor waterfall and everything. But the whole thing was drugs and drinking, and of course he was a complete freak when it came to sex. You can't

imagine. But I wasn't going to do all those things. I mean,
I loved him.

HUMBERT

What things?

LOLITA

You know — weird, filthy things. Two girls and two boys,
and three or four men, and Vivian filming the whole thing.
I said, no, I'm not going to blow all those beastly boys —
I want you and only you. I was nuts for him, I really was.
So he threw me out. Oh, I love this song.

*She cocks her ear toward Dick's radio, which is playing something
sweet and sad. For a moment she closes her eyes and sways to the
tune. Humbert stares at her, at her ropy hands and white arms and
her enormous belly. The music fills the room.*

HUMBERT'S VOICE

I looked and looked at her, and I knew, as clearly as I
know that I will die, that I loved her more than anything I
had ever seen or imagined on earth. She was only the
dead-leaf echo of the nymphet from long ago — but I
loved her, this Lolita, pale and polluted and big with
another man's child. She could fade and wither — I didn't
care. I would still go mad with tenderness at the mere
sight of her face.

HUMBERT

Lolita, I just have to say this. From here to that old car
you know so well is a stretch of twenty-five paces. Make
those twenty-five steps. With me. Now.

LOLITA

You're saying you'll give us the money if I go to a motel
with you?

HUMBERT

No, no, no. I mean leave here now, and come live with
me. And die with me, and everything with me.

LOLITA
You're crazy.

HUMBERT
If you refuse, you still get the money.

LOLITA
No kidding?

He hands her an envelope. She tears it open and gasps.

LOLITA
You're giving us four thousand bucks?

Humbert bursts into tears. He covers his face, sobbing. She touches his wrist.

HUMBERT
No. Don't touch me. I'll die if you touch me. Is there no hope of your coming with me? Tell me.

LOLITA
No, honey, no. I'd almost rather — oops.

She drops the envelope on the floor. Time stands still. She bends to pick it up. As she does, he speaks, half-sobbing, almost to himself.

HUMBERT
Did you call me honey?

LOLITA
Listen, I think it's really great of you to give us all this dough. It makes everything possible for Dick and me. Oh, don't cry. Let me get you another beer. Want another beer?

HUMBERT
Lo.

LOLITA
Look, I'm sorry I cheated so much, but that's the way
things are, okay? Stop crying, okay?

*Humbert stands, goes to the window, takes a few deep breaths, and
stops crying.*

HUMBERT
I'll go.

LOLITA
Can I call Dick to say goodbye?

HUMBERT
No. I don't want to see him at all, at all.

*They walk toward the door and look out. Humbert smiles a little
through his tears.*

HUMBERT
The old car. Remember?

LOLITA
It's looking kind of purplish around the gills.

The dog joins them and starts barking. Lolita moves toward Humbert as if to give him a little goodbye peck. He jerks away. He looks at her.

HUMBERT
Lo, can you ever forget what I've done to you?

Lolita looks at him for a moment. Then down at the dog.

LOLITA
Say goodbye, Molly. Say goodbye to my dad.

Humbert walks down the steps and gets into the car. In the background Lolita calls, "Hey, Dick! Guess what?"

Humbert watches her go around the house toward the back yard. He starts the car and drives slowly down the street. The dog follows, woofing at the car.

HUMBERT'S CAR — DRIVING — NIGHT   *Moths in the headlights.*
Dark barns. A drive-in movie with a gigantic screen, slanting away
among the fields. A figure on the screen raises a film-noir gun, pre-
pares to shoot — and then passing trees obscure the view.

HUMBERT'S CAR — EARLY MORNING   *Humbert reaches into the*
glove compartment and takes out his gun, which is bandaged up like
a maimed limb. He has over-oiled it, and the black oil gets all over
his hands. He pushes a cartridge magazine into its butt. He wraps a
handful of spare bullets in a rag and puts them in his pocket. Then,
as he goes to close the glove compartment, a glint catches his eye.
It is a three-year-old bobby pin, covered with dust. He picks it up,
looks at it lovingly, blows the dust off it, and places it carefully on the
dashboard.

He grabs a gin bottle sitting on the seat by his side, and takes a long
swig.

Nearby is a gate opening onto a long, woodsy driveway. A sign says:
"Pavor Manor." Humbert drives up the driveway.

Brilliant sunlight through his windshield. Birds shriek and dive. He
stops the car among the trees. He pats the gun in his pocket, grasps
the bottle of gin, and takes one more long drink. He gets out and
walks toward the door. He rings the bell.

Silence. He tries the knocker.

Silence. He pushes the door. It creaks open.

Inside, a spacious and ugly hall. Humbert creeps in, hand on pocket,
peering about him. In an adjacent drawing room, signs of tumult,
glasses on the carpet, empty bottles, dirty ashtrays and plates.

Humbert trudges up the gloomy staircase. He reaches the landing
and begins to creep down the corridor. He passes a library full of
flowers. He passes a bare room with mirrors and a polar bear skin
rug. He goes down the hall, looking into empty rooms, and locking

them with the keys he finds sticking out of keyholes. The keys jingle in his pockets as he walks.

A bathroom door. Humbert approaches it. He hears a flushing sound, and Quilty comes out, wearing a purple bathrobe. He walks past Humbert without seeming to notice him. He goes down the stairs. Humbert follows.

Quilty wanders through the house, oblivious. Humbert follows, his step drunken and springy, a cartoonish exaggeration of a hunter's stalking gait. He crunches a cocktail glass underfoot.

Finally, in an Oriental parlor, Quilty turns and faces Humbert.

QUILTY
Now who are you? Are you by any chance Brewster?

HUMBERT
If you like.

Quilty looks pleased. They sit, Humbert holding the gun.

QUILTY
You know, you don't look like Jack Brewster. I mean, the resemblance is not particularly striking. Somebody told me he had a brother with the same phone company.

HUMBERT
I am neither of the Brewsters.

QUILTY
Oh. So you haven't come to bother me about those long-distance calls? People — I'm not accusing you, Brewster, I'm talking about people in general. They come in without even knocking, and they use the kitchen, they use the phone. Phil calls Philadelphia. Pat calls Patagonia. I refuse to pay.

HUMBERT
Quilty, do you recall a little girl named Dolores Haze? Dolly Haze?

QUILTY
Sure. She could have made a few calls. Who cares?

HUMBERT
I do, Quilty. You see, I am her father.

A look of recognition flickers in Quilty's eyes.

QUILTY
Nonsense. You're a foreigner. You're an agent of a foreign power. You're a foreign literary agent.

HUMBERT
She was my child.

QUILTY
I'm very fond of children myself. And fathers — I love fathers.

Beating his pockets, Quilty attempts to rise from his seat.

HUMBERT
Down!

Quilty sits.

QUILTY
Don't roar at me, Brewster. I'm dying for a smoke.

HUMBERT
You're dying anyway.

QUILTY
Look, you're beginning to bore me. Why don't you —
Say, that's a swell little gun you've got there. What do you want for her?

Quilty stretches his hand toward the gun, and Humbert slaps it down. They knock over a box on a low table, and Drome cigarettes fall out.

Quilty picks one up.

QUILTY

Got a light?

HUMBERT

Quilty, I want you to concentrate. You're about to die.

Quilty is pulling apart the cigarette and munching bits of the tobacco.

Humbert points the gun at the carpet and pulls the trigger. The gun clicks. Quilty looks at his foot, at the pistol, at his foot. Humbert pulls the trigger again. The gun goes off, but the bullet enters the rug.

QUILTY

Give me that thing, for Christ's sake.

Quilty reaches for the gun. Humbert pushes him back in the chair.

Lolita

HUMBERT
Do you want to be executed sitting or standing?

QUILTY
Ah, let me think. Not an easy question.

HUMBERT
Try to understand what is happening to you.

QUILTY
Listen, I made a mistake. Which I regret — sincerely. You
see, I didn't even have any fun with your Dolly. I am practically impotent, to tell you the melancholy truth.
(feeling sorry for himself)
I did give her a splendid vacation. She met some remarkable people. Do you happen to know —

*Suddenly Quilty lurches forward on top of Humbert, sending the pis-
tol hurtling under a chest of drawers. Humbert shoves him back in*

his chair. Quilty puffs a little and folds his arms. Humbert, watching him to see how groggy he really is, begins to stoop toward the chest of drawers. He stoops and glances. Quilty is still, yet watching him carefully. Humbert risks another little stoop. Quilty sighs impatiently.

QUILTY
My dear sir, stop trifling with life and death. I am a widely acclaimed playwright. I know all the ropes when it comes to melodrama. So why don't you just let me handle this? What happens now is that I fetch a poker and then we can fish out your little property.

As he says this, he slowly rises, feigning nonchalance. But Humbert's eye catches a glint of the gun peeking from beneath the chest, and both of them dive for it. They roll all over the floor. Quilty is naked under his robe. For a moment, he almost suffocates Humbert. Finally Humbert retrieves the gun.

The two of them sit, panting hard, looking at each other. Humbert points the gun at Quilty.

HUMBERT
Stay still.

QUILTY
Now look here, Mac. You are drunk, and I am a sick man. I need a nurse. To nurse my impotence. Listen, we are both men of the world. If you bear me a grudge, I am ready to make amends.

HUMBERT
You cheated me of my redemption. You have to die.

QUILTY
I have no idea what you're talking about. Really, you have to admit you were never an ideal stepfather. I didn't force your little protegee to join me. It was she who made me remove her to a happier home. Now look. See this house? Not as modern as that ranch she and I shared with dear friends, but it's roomy, cool in the summer, very

comfortable. I suggest you move in. I'll retire to England or Florence or somewhere, and this place is yours, gratis. Under the condition you stop pointing that fucking gun at me.

                    HUMBERT
Do you have anything serious to say before dying?

                    QUILTY
Drop that gun. By the way, I don't know if you care for the bizarre, but if you do, I can offer you as a house pet a rather exciting little freak, a lady with three breasts, one a dandy — drop that gun. I think you'll be happy here. We have a most reliable and bribable charwoman — cleaning lady is the American term. She has not only daughters but granddaughters, and I know a thing or two about the chief of police that makes him my slave. Drop that gun. Oh, another thing — you're going to like this. I have an absolutely unique collection of erotica upstairs — drop that gun — and moreover I can arrange for you to attend

executions. Not everybody knows the chair is painted yellow —

Humbert fires. The bullet hits a black rocking chair, causing it to rock madly. In an instant, Quilty is up and out of the room, wiggling his fingers in the air.

MUSIC ROOM   *Quilty rushes into the music room, and he and Humbert tug at the door, Quilty trying to close it and Humbert struggling to open it.*

Humbert wins, whereupon Quilty careers over to the piano, sits down and plays several hysterical chords. Humbert fires again, and this time he hits Quilty in the side. Quilty rises, his head thrown back in a howl.

Quilty hurtles himself into the hall. Humbert follows.

Quilty, suddenly dignified and morose, walks up the stairs. Humbert shoots four more times, and hits Quilty every time. With each hit, Quilty's face twitches as if he were exaggerating the pain, and he shivers. As the two of them proceed, Quilty mutters under his breath in a fake British accent.

> QUILTY
>
> Ah, that hurts, sir . . . Ah, that hurts atrociously, my
> dear fellow . . . Ah — very painful, very painful indeed.
> Yes . . . .Ah, God, you should not continue in this fashion,
> really.

Quilty reaches the landing but staggers on. Humbert climbs the stairs, reloading. His hands are bloody and black with oil from the gun. Quilty trudges from room to room, bleeding majestically. Humbert follows him. Quilty is still muttering.

> QUILTY
>
> Well, I think we've had quite enough of that for one day,
> haven't we?

Humbert fires again and hits Quilty in the head.

MASTER BEDROOM   *Quilty enters with a burst of royal purple where his ear had been. He curls up in his bed, wrapping the chaotic bedclothes about him.*

> QUILTY
> *(coughing and spitting)*
> Get out! Get out of here!

Humbert fires and hits Quilty through the bedclothes. A big pink bubble forms in Quilty's mouth and suddenly vanishes. We watch Humbert's face as he watches Quilty die. Humbert sinks into a chair. He looks blank, awed. Flies perch on Quilty's head. Humbert looks down. He is holding one of Quilty's slippers as though it were a gun. He tosses it aside and feels under him — he has been sitting on the gun. He looks at it.

Gradually he becomes aware of a hum of voices and radio music. He goes out of the room.

STAIR LANDING   *Humbert looks down to the first floor. In the hall and sitting room are a fat man in an easy chair and two dark-haired pale young girls, side by side on a davenport. A red-faced man is emerging from the kitchen, carrying glasses. In the kitchen three other women are chatting. Humbert descends the stairs. He looks monstrous. The visitors observe him with mild curiosity.*

HUMBERT

I have just killed Clare Quilty.

RED-FACED MAN

Good for you.

FAT MAN

Someone ought to have done it long ago.

FADED BLONDE

What's he saying, Tony?

RED-FACED MAN

Says he's killed Cue.

FADED BLONDE

Good. One of these days, I will too.

FAT MAN

We all should, really.

General chuckling.

RED-FACED MAN

Anyway, he'd better come down if we're going to get to that game.

FAT MAN

Give Killer here a drink.

The two girls on the davenport smile at Humbert.

GIRL
Want a drink, Killer?

Humbert stares at them for a moment, coming to his senses.

HUMBERT
No, thank you. Thank you all the same.

He staggers out of the room, out of the house.

There are rows of cars parked outside now, and Humbert has to squeeze between them to get into the old blue Melmoth. He begins to drive down the Pavor Manor driveway.

NEW ENGLAND COUNTRYSIDE — DAY   *We are at the beginning again. The Melmoth drives slowly just outside a small town. It creeps over into the left lane, where it zig-zags very evenly. Cars come at it, then swerve into the opposite lane, honking.*

INTERSECTION IN A SMALL TOWN   *The light turns red, but the Melmoth sails through it.*

The gun sits on the seat next to Humbert. We look up to his hands on the steering wheel. Between his right thumb and index finger, the bobby pin.

POLICE CRUISER   *Two cops inside. The driver slides the radio microphone back in its holster, glances at his partner, and guns the engine.*

BEHIND A BILLBOARD   *Two motorcycle cops give a sharp nod and pull onto the highway.*

HUMBERT'S CAR   *It weaves as cars swerve to avoid him. Sound of the wind.*
HUMBERT'S REAR-VIEW MIRROR   *A line of cops, some in cruisers some on motorbikes.*

A ROADBLOCK   *Humbert sees it, nods to himself, and drives gently off the road, his car bumping up a huge green hill.*

He lurches with the bumps, smiling a little, almost as though the bumpiness gave him pleasure.

A HERD OF COWS.   *They look up in mild surprise as Humbert's car boings to a halt in their midst. Humbert gets out, and, staggering slightly, makes his way a few steps beyond the cows to the top of a hill.*

He sees a valley: a little town, fields, behind them great timbered mountains. Small grasshoppers spurt out of roadside weeds. Lights are beginning to twinkle as dusk falls, and we hear children in the square below. Their sound rises.

Humbert stands still.

HUMBERT
(half whispering)

Lo-li-ta.

We pull back to see the police coming up the hill behind him.

The sound of the children rises until it is all we hear.

BLACK SCREEN   *We still hear the children, and then Humbert's*
voice:

HUMBERT

What I heard then was the melody of children at play, nothing but that. And I knew that the hopelessly poignant thing was not Lolita's absence from my side, but the absence of her voice from that chorus. And now I make the following decision with all the legal impact of a signed testament: I wish this memoir to be made public only when Lolita and I are both dead. Thus neither of us is alive when these words are heard. Yet the blood is still throbbing in my veins as I speak them. So I can still wish you well, Lolita, the way a father would, from here to Alaska. Be true to your husband. Do not let other fellows touch you. Do not talk to strangers. I hope you will love your baby. I hope it will be a boy. That husband of yours, I hope, will always treat you well, because otherwise my ghost will come at him like black smoke, like a demented giant, and pull him apart nerve by nerve. And do not pity Clare Quilty. One had to choose between him and Humbert, and one wanted Humbert to exist at least a couple of months longer, so as to have him make you live in the minds of later generations. For this is the only immortality you and I may share, my Lolita.

TITLE:

HUMBERT DIED OF A CORONARY THROMBOSIS ON
NOVEMBER 16, 1950.

LOLITA DIED IN CHILDBIRTH ON CHRISTMAS DAY, 1950.

THE END

ABOUT THE AUTHOR

Stephen Schiff is a staff writer for The New Yorker magazine, where he writes feature-length cultural profiles, essays, and criticism. Lolita was his first screenplay, but he has continued as an active screenwriter. His adaptation of the best-seller The Deep End of the Ocean was filmed by Ulu Grosbard at Sony Pictures for release in September, 1998; it stars Michelle Pfeiffer, Treat Williams, and Whoopi Goldberg. His screenplay True Crime was directed by Clint Eastwood, whom it also stars; the Warner Bros. production began filming in May, 1998. He has also been signed to write screenplays for Robert de Niro and Quincy Jones, Mike Nichols, and Barry Sonnenfeld. He lives in New York City with his wife and daughter.